ALL IS

ALL IS

*Hardbound Gift Edition

ANN MARIE STEWART

ALL IS

Calm

ALL IS

Bright

For the Heart of Christmas

PUBLISHERS

ALL IS *Calm,* ALL IS *Bright*
for the Heart of Christmas

Published by AMG Publishers. All Rights Reserved.

Published in association with the literary agency of MacGregor and Luedeke, P.O. Box 1316, Manzanita, OR 97130

Editing and typesetting by Rick Steele Editorial Services, Ringgold, GA (https://steeleeditorialservices.myportfolio.com)

Cover Design by Jonathan Lewis of Jonlin Creative, Pekin, Illinois

Printed in Canada

Dedicated to my friend Carrie Leslie

About the Author

ANN MARIE STEWART is the Christy Award® winning author of *Stars in the Grass*, followed up by the Ippy Award winning *Out of the Water*, and is at work on *REMNANTS*, a memoir about her grandparents' escape from Russia in 1929.

Ann has also authored *Preparing My Heart for Advent*, *Preparing My Heart for Easter*, and *Preparing My Heart for Motherhood*, and writes the column "Ann's Lovin' Ewe" for *The Country Register*. Ann combines her experience in education, musical theatre, and film and television to dramatize her writing. In addition, Ann teaches voice out of her home in Virginia, where she and her husband raised two daughters, and lots of sheep on Skye Moor Farm.

The following Christmas carols featured in *All Is Calm, All Is Bright* and recorded by Ann Marie Stewart, as well as the three Christmas pageants, can be found on her website: www.AnnMarieStewart.com

Christmas Carols Featured:
Come, Thou Long Expected Jesus
O Come O Come Emmanuel
O Little Town of Bethlehem
Angels We Have Heard on High
Hark the Herald Angels Sing
Silent Night
What Child Is This
The Holly and the Ivy
We Three Kings
Lully, Lullay Thou Little Tiny Child
Thou Didst Leave Thy Throne
Joy to the World
O Come All Ye Faithful

Christmas Pageants Featured:

- ***Happy Birthday, Jesus***
  When Jesus asks about the night he was born, Mary tells him all about the wondrous event, dramatized by actors.

- ***The Nativity Alive***
  After neighborhood carolers steal the baby Jesus from an outdoor nativity set, one child lingers and meets the elderly owner who brings each figurine to life to tell the Christmas story.

- ***Come to the Manger***
  As a family races out the door to their annual Church Christmas pageant, the "star," shepherd, and reluctant Bethlehem villager suddenly find

themselves transported back to Bethlehem where they meet the true characters and play different roles.

Many thanks to beta readers: Carrie Leslie, Lydia Harris, Louise Jane Eskew, Julia Tomiak, Maureen Erickson, Celeste Miller, Lori Galloway, Karyl Groeneveld, Joan McClenny, Jackie Pettit Forrest, Heidi Veldman, Laura Roden, Ginny Oustad.

As a child I lay on the carpet studying the 1950's vintage mica and glitter cardboard village beneath my grandmother's Christmas tree. I moved the people around and imagined what they were doing and where they were going. They were all happy and full of the Christmas spirit. It was such a perfect snow-globe-like world.

Once a "grown up," I still wanted a vintage village under our family tree, and so, piece by piece, our Studio 56® Snow Village grew. Now my adult daughter Christine comes home and sets up the snow, lights, churches and houses, skating rink, and sledding hill, along with the happy, festive villagers. Her perfect nostalgic village begs us to visit.

Except it's not real. And like the houses in our Snow Village, sometimes we all dress up on the outside to be holiday perfect when no outward décor can bring about an inner peace.

"Calm and bright" is what I'd like for December. A time to celebrate and focus on the Prince of Peace and the Light of the World. To return to the heart of Christmas.

All Is Calm, All Is Bright will take you through the Christmas story with December devotionals focusing on Immanuel, God with Us, as we make our way to the manger. Each devotional's title is taken from that day's scripture. You can have fun finding it in the text.

May I suggest that throughout this Advent season, you give yourself permission to scale back. Simplify your calendar so that you can take time for what's really important. Invest in people and experiences. and decorations. Love, patience, and kindness matter more than perfect lights, a clean house, and the tallest spruce in the window. Rethink gift giving by sharing one or two meaningful presents and being fully present with others. Keep the nativity at the heart. On page 135 you can even find the Christmas story in chronological order.

These simplifications can reduce stress and busyness and create new "calm and bright" traditions.

Dear Lord, I long for us all to have a Christmas with You as our Light and You as our Peace. This Christmas, may we clothe ourselves with compassion, kindness, humility, gentleness, and patience. May we be peacemakers, and may we bear with each other and forgive whatever grievances we have against one another. Help us forgive as You forgave us. And over all these things, may we put on love, which binds them all together in perfect unity (based on Colossians 3:12-14).

Come, Thou Long Expected Jesus

My soul faints with longing for your salvation,
but I have put my hope in your word. (Psalm 119:81)

"How many days until Christmas?" My girls were not allowed to ask that question until December 1st. It's too similar to the recurring pleas of the "When will we get there?" whine from the backseat of a long car journey.

Advent or "the coming" is a journey, a time to wait, anticipate, and prepare our hearts for the coming of Jesus. It's much more than a one-day celebration, it's a month to rest in the Lord, and remember the God of our past, present, and future. In anticipating His first coming, we celebrate His presence in the present, and look for His second coming to earth.

Although the story of Christmas is primarily recorded in the New Testament, the Old Testament has much to say about Jesus, ending with the Book of Malachi and the promise of restoration and healing.

> *"But for you who revere my name, the sun of righteousness*
> *will rise with healing in its rays. And you will go out and frolic*
> *like well-fed calves."* (Malachi 4:2)

But between the Old and New Testaments, between Malachi and Matthew, there's four hundred years of waiting for Christ's birth as Israel longs for a Savior. The Christmas carol "Come, Thou Long Expected Jesus" describes the people of old yearning for someone to free them from fears, sins, and ultimately, someone to give them a much-needed rest.

Maybe the song is a prayer for all of us, too. We long to be set free from our fears. We yearn to be forgiven. And oh, how we need Jesus, who says,

> *Come to me, all you who are weary and burdened, and I will give you rest. Take my yoke upon you and learn from me, for I am gentle and humble in heart, and you will find rest for your souls.* (Matthew 11:28–29)

"Come, Thou Long Expected Jesus" declares why Jesus was born and that Advent is a time to celebrate His coming to earth, His coming to reign in our hearts, and His second coming, when we will be raised to His glorious throne to live with Him forever. And that, my friend, is the best part! With a hope like that, we realize Christmas is one day, but Advent anticipates eternity.

Come, Thou Long Expected Jesus
Come, Thou long expected Jesus, Born to set thy people free;
From our fears and sins release us, Let us find our rest in Thee.
Israel's Strength and Consolation, Hope of all the earth Thou art;

Dear desire of every nation, Joy of every longing heart.
Born thy people to deliver, Born a child and yet a King.
Born to reign in us forever, Now Thy gracious Kingdom bring.
By Thine own eternal Spirit, Rule in all our hearts alone;
By Thine all-sufficient merit, Raise us to thy glorious throne.
During Advent, set aside a familiar time and place in your
home where you can come each day to relax with a hot cup
of tea or coffee. Settle into your favorite sofa, throw over a
blanket, and feel the love God sends to us. Contemplate the
long-expected Jesus who was born a child and yet a King.
Discover the calm in prayer and the bright in the excitement
of His first and second coming.

How many days until Christmas? You're now allowed to ask. There's 24! Let the birthday celebrations begin as we await His glorious arrival.

> *"In that day the Root of Jesse will stand as a banner for the*
> *peoples; the nations will rally to him, and his resting place*
> *will be glorious." (Isaiah 11:10)*

Prayer

Heavenly Father, I long to celebrate Christmas because
it is the birth of Your Son. May Your Son be the joy of my
longing heart. He is Israel's strength and consolation, and He
is mine, too. Jesus is the rest for my soul. He was born a child
and yet a king, born to set us free and to deliver us, born to
reign in us forever. Thank You for sending Him to earth.

Fixing Our Eyes upon Jesus

As for God, his way is perfect:

*The L*ord's *word is flawless;*

he shields all who take refuge in him. (2 Samuel 22:31)

Our historic Virginia church on Main Street with its stained-glass windows, white columns, and wrap-around balcony, was decorated with greenery, candles, and a Chrismon tree. And on this special Sunday evening, the sanctuary was packed with parents and visitors eager to watch their children shine as characters in the Christmas story. After costume fittings, weeks of rehearsals, and learning lines, my preschool and elementary cast of shepherds, wise men, angels, and stable animals were ready to perform in the annual Christmas pageant.

Or so I hoped.

The pageant began with a nervous fourth grader narrating, "And a decree went forth from Sy uh REE uh..." she said, struggling with the pronunciation. We all felt her hesitation, including a preschooler dressed as a nativity rooster who belted out, "DY-uh-ree uh?" Giggles resounded from the rest of the preschool barnyard of sheep, donkeys, roosters, and cows. The audience nervously joined in the laughter. That was only the beginning.

Things got worse when the angels began fighting in the balcony. Prior to the performance, my assistant director suggested that because the kindergarten and first grade angels were unsure of their song, I should have my angelic daughter Christine sing directly into the Angel of the LORD's mike to bolster the multitude of heavenly host. I told Christine to stand next to Mason (the Angel of the LORD) and, after he had announced, "Fear not, I bring you glad tidings of great joy!" to take over the mike.

However, I forgot to tell Mason.

As head angel, first-grader Mason was not going to allow kindergartener Christine any time on his mike. Mason rubbed the feathers off Christine's furry white wings as he bumped her away and crowded his haloed head into his mike. Wings flapped, and the angel chorus nearly took flight. "Gloria! Gloria!" the other angels sang as two microphoned angels fought hard over their own glory.

I continued conducting the song from below, my flailing arms imitating the angelic ones above. What else could I do? Christine was doing exactly what she was supposed to do, and my Angel of the Lord had been taught that choir members should never sing directly into the mike unless performing a solo—especially not the angel of the Lord's mike! The audience howled with laughter as they watched the battle in the heavenly places. For many, it was the highlight of that year's Christmas pageant.

What will be your Christmas highlight? Probably not a perfectly planned party or the photoshopped Instagram-worthy moment. We can enjoy the holidays more by letting all that go and looking to perfection only in Him. Nothing will be perfect except the One having the birthday. While the world celebrates the holidays, return to the holy days, and keep your eyes fixed on Jesus.

What can prompt you to keep your mind fixed on Him? To take in a deep breath and inhale His peace and exhale anything that detracts? Consider writing out the verse below and posting it somewhere in your home.

> *fixing our eyes on Jesus, the pioneer and perfecter of faith. For the joy set before him he endured the cross, scorning its shame, and sat down at the right hand of the throne of God.* (Hebrews 12:2)

Prayer

Dear Jesus—May my day begin with my eyes fixed on You. No matter what happens today, help me to keep my eyes focused on You, the author and perfecter of my faith. Remind me that by coming to earth as a babe, you set aside the joy and endured the cross. Now you sit at the right hand of the throne of God, and I can close my eyes and picture you there. In Jesus's name.

And His Name Shall Be Called

*She will give birth to a son, and you are to give him the
name Jesus, because he will save his people from their sins.
(Matthew 1:21)*

My maiden name was a string of thirteen letters impossible to pronounce. As a substitute teacher, my introductory trick included turning my back on my students to write across the blackboard R-O-E-T-C-I-S-O-E-N-D-E-R while the classroom quieted in awe. They were forgiving when I took roll and mispronounced a name or two.

One good thing about growing up with that name was that everybody knew all my relatives. One bad thing about growing up with that name was that everybody knew all my relatives. And so, as a Roetcisoender (<u>RITZ</u>-ah-cinder) I wanted to make sure I represented my family well.

When we named our firstborn daughter, we wanted her name to have meaning. Christine Alane means "Bright and shining follower of Christ." Which is exactly how we hope she lives her life.

Throughout the Bible, names hold meaning. Some of these characters live up (or down) to their name! Zechariah (Yah remembers), Elizabeth (God of Oath), Abraham, (father of a great multitude), Ruth (friend), Nabal (fool), Mordecai (strong or bitter), and David (beloved).

It's intriguing that the significance of Jacob's name (deceiver, heel catcher) is acknowledged by his twin brother Esau: "Isn't he rightly named Jacob? This is the second time he has taken advantage of me: He took my birthright, and now he's taken my blessing!" (Genesis 27:36)

Isaiah 9:6 prophesies about Jesus' name, its meaning, and His roles: "And his name shall be called Wonderful Counselor, Mighty God, Everlasting Father, Prince of Peace.

Jesus' Father in heaven then told Jesus's father on earth exactly what to name him. His earthly name of *Yeshu'a* means *Yahweh saves,* and Jesus means *The Lord is Salvation.* At the announcement of Jesus's birth, the angel proclaimed three titles, all revealing aspects of Jesus and the plan for His life.

> *"For unto you is born this day in the city of David a **Savior**, who is Christ the Lord. (Luke 2:11 ESV, emphasis added)*

There are a lot of names packed in that verse and they all have meaning.

Savior	Deliverer
Christ/Messiah	Anointed one
Lord	Authority and power

But this is no ordinary name. *This* name is above all names.

> Far above all rule and authority and power and dominion,
> and above every name that is named, not only in this age
> but also in the one to come. (Ephesians 1:21)

Yes, the name of Jesus is above all names, and His rule and power is for eternity. Why?

"There is salvation in no one else, for there is no other name under heaven given among men by which we must be saved." (Acts 4:12)

No other name but Jesus saves. *Jesus Christ* combines his mortal, earthly name with his title. How are we to react to the name of *Jesus Christ*? Not as an expletive, exclamation of amazement, or acronym, but as Lord and King.

> Therefore God has highly exalted him and bestowed on him
> the name that is above every name, so that at the name of
> Jesus every knee should bow, in heaven and on earth and
> under the earth, and every tongue confess that Jesus Christ
> is Lord, to the glory of God the Father. (Philippians 2:9-11)

Every time you hear the name of Jesus this Christmas season, consider how His name is precious not just because of His birth, but because of His life, death, and resurrection. And remember, we bear His name when we call ourselves Christians, followers of Christ.

Prayer

Jesus, Your name is above all names. You are Savior, Messiah, and Lord. You are my deliverer, You are anointed, You have power and authority, You are my Preserver. I confess that You are Lord to the glory of God the Father. I know there is no other name under heaven by which I can be saved. I call upon You, Jesus. Help me, as a follower of You, as a Christian, to bear your name well. In Jesus's all-powerful name, Amen.

The Word of the Prophets

And we have the word of the prophets made more certain,
and you will do well to pay attention to it, as to a light
shining in a dark place, until the day dawns and the morning
star rises in your hearts. (2 Peter 1:19)

If you Google: *Finding Jesus in Every Book of the Bible*
(https://www.biblestudytools.com/bible-study/topical-stud-
ies/in-every-book-of-the-bible.html), you'll learn how Jesus
is mentioned throughout the Old Testament, whether in
creation, in types and symbols, foreshadowing, and even
the design of the tabernacle. In addition, there are also
more than three hundred Old Testament prophecies about
Christ that are then fulfilled in the New Testament.

In John 5:46, Jesus even confirms his Old Testament
presence. "If you believed Moses, you would believe me,
for he wrote about me." What did Moses write? Included in
Moses' five books are the sacrifice of Isaac, Passover Lamb,
Bread from heaven, the bronze snake, the rock that was
struck, and the promise of a prophet like Moses.

I'm not listing all three hundred today, but here are three
prophecies.

"Therefore the Lord Himself will give you a sign: The virgin
will be with child and will give birth to a son, and will call
him Immanuel." (Isaiah 7:14)

> But you, Bethlehem Ephrathah, though you are small among
> the clans of Judah, out of you will come for me one who
> will be ruler over Israel, whose origins are from of old, from
> ancient times. (Micah 5:2)

> Nations will come to your light, and kings to the brightness
> of your dawn. (Isaiah 60:3)

Yesterday we read how Old Testament prophecy offers
titles for Jesus: Immanuel, Wonderful Counselor, Mighty
God, Prince of Peace. It's beautiful to learn, understand, and
pray these titles or even to sing them!

The Christmas carol "O Come O Come Emmanuel" is a
source for Jesus's Old Testament names. As you read
through them or listen to the carol, make note of these
titles.

O come, O come, <u>Emmanuel</u>,
And ransom captive Israel
That mourns in lonely exile here
Until the <u>Son of God</u> appear.

Refrain:
Rejoice! Rejoice! Emmanuel
Shall come to thee, O Israel.
O come, Thou <u>Wisdom from on high</u>,
Who orders all things mightily;
To us the path of knowledge show,
And teach us in its ways to go.

O come, Thou <u>Branch of Jesse's</u> stem,
Unto Thine own and rescue them!
From depths of hell Thy people save,
And give them vict'ry o'er the grave.
O come, Thou <u>Key of David</u>, come
And open wide our heav'nly home;
Make safe for us the heav'nward road,
And bar the way to death's abode.
O come, Thou <u>Bright and Morning Star</u>,
And bring us comfort from afar!
Dispel the shadows of the night
And turn our darkness into light.
O come, <u>Desire of nations</u>, bind
In one the hearts of all mankind;
Bid all our sad divisions cease,
And be Thyself our <u>King of Peace</u>.

For the Old Testament prophecies and promises, there are New Testament fulfillments, confirmations, and a big "Yes" in Jesus Christ. Because we can study both testaments, we are privileged, as in the scripture heading, to have "the word of the prophets made more certain." And we should pay attention to it.

Try Googling Jesus in the Old Testament, and as you find Him, exclaim AMEN!

> *"For no matter how many promises God has made, they are 'YES' in Christ. And so through him the 'Amen' is spoken by us to the glory of God." (2 Corinthians 1:20)*

Prayer

Jesus, You are wisdom from on high, the Branch of Jesse's stem, Key of David, Bright and Morning Star, Desire of Nations, King of Peace. I yearn to know more about the prophecies, promises, and the fulfillment. Help me see you in the Old and New Testament and learn how to be more Christ-like.

The Beginning of the Good News

*The beginning of the Good News about Jesus the Messiah,
the Son of God (Mark 1:1)*

Many have undertaken to draw up an account of the
things that have been fulfilled among us, just as they
were handed down to us by those who from the first were
eyewitnesses and servants of the word. With this in mind,
since I myself have carefully investigated everything from
the beginning, I too decided to write an orderly account for
you, most excellent Theophilus, so that you may know the
certainty of the things you have been taught. (Luke 1:1-4)

One December, Jeff's teacher encouraged the parents of
her students to share their holiday traditions with her
second-grade class. His mother, Caroline, volunteered to
explain how our extended family dramatizes the nativity
each Christmas Eve. When Jeff's teacher only wanted secular
traditions, Caroline explained that leaving Jesus out would
confuse her son, Jeff.

After the teacher reluctantly agreed, Caroline brought a nativity set and several costumes, explaining how the eight
cousins dress and act out the story. A new baby in the
family plays Baby Jesus, and some little ones are costumed as
sheep or a star.

"Christmas is about a birthday party—Jesus' birthday," she began. "When Jesus was born, many guests came to His party," she continued. "Joseph was there, and Jesus's mother, Mary, was there." Then Jeff's baby sister blurted out, "But Joseph isn't Jesus' daddy!" and Caroline thought she'd never be asked back again.

"Joseph is Mary's husband," Caroline continued as she pulled out a shepherd's cloak and a Magi's crown. "The shepherds left their sheep and came to the birthday party, and wise men came bringing gifts." The children watched in wonder, fascinated with a birthday party so dissimilar to their own. "When Jeff played Baby Jesus in our church Christmas pageant, he was very quiet until the organ played 'Silent Night,' and scared him so badly he began screaming." The children enjoyed the story and laughed.

That year Caroline bore witness that Christmas is a celebration of Jesus' birth and introduced some children to the Christ child.

The first four authors of the New Testament bear witness of Christ, but from different perspectives and write to different audiences.

Matthew, the Jewish tax collector, emphasizes Jesus as King to an audience of Jews. Missionary Mark emphasizes Christ as Savior, spending almost half of his story in Christ's last week on earth and addressing an audience of Jewish Christians. Doctor Luke emphasizes Jesus as the Son of Man to Gentiles. John declares "In the beginning was the Word, and the Word was with God, and the Word was God," repeatedly declaring how God and Jesus are ONE. Each disciple shares the gospel, or good news, in his own special way.

In our own special way, each one of us, through our actions and our words, also bring a unique perspective to the re-telling of the Christmas story. The gospel is the greatest gift of Christmas as well as the greatest gift we can share with others. Through our Christmas letter, simple hospitality, decorations and music in our home, invitation to a Christmas event, or perhaps our own neighborhood re-staging of the Christmas story, we can help share the good news and truth of the Season.

> How beautiful on the mountains are the feet of those who bring good news, who proclaim peace, who bring good tidings who proclaim salvation who say to Zion, "Your God reigns!" (Isaiah 52:7)

Prayer

God, give me the opportunity to tell someone about Christmas. May I proclaim peace and salvation and bring good tidings to others. Holy Spirit, give me the words to share the good news. Jesus, may I always be ready to share the good news that You came to earth to save us from our sins and reconcile us to God.

Born of God

> Yet to all who received him, to those who believed in his name, he gave the right to become children of God—children born not of natural descent, nor of human decision or a husband's will, but born of God (John 1:12-13).

I love a good adoption story. I'm fascinated with why, where, and how the pieces fit together to form a beautiful whole.

After Jeff and Jill adopted their baby boy, James, they soon received a call from their international adoption agency telling them, "Your little girl from China is ready!" Jeff and Jill's papers were "mistakenly" not put on hold. After looking at the little girl's file, they were off to China in the middle of a typhoon to adopt Lydia, an eighteen-month-old with the same birth date as her six-month-old baby brother, James. There was no "mistake"—Lydia belongs in their family.

Barbara and Tripp already had nine children when they adopted. Their eighth child was born with Down Syndrome and so increased their heart and love capacity that they adopted three more boys with Down Syndrome. All these children were chosen, loved, named, and adopted. There's nothing better than an adoption story with a happy ending!

Mary's husband, Joseph, is Jesus's adoptive dad. And when we believe in Jesus, we, too, are adopted children of God, heirs through Christ.

Who wouldn't want to cry out "Daddy! Daddy!" and run into the arms of a loving God who longs to nurture and give His children good things? How wonderful to be the apple of God's eye or nestle under the shadow of His wing. And similarly, what father doesn't delight in hearing, "Daddy! Daddy!" as his child runs for a warm embrace? God must love to hear us call!

Like the children from these stories, when we are adopted, we experience change. We are loved, chosen, given the name "Child of God" and we retain that title for eternity. Embrace that title as you celebrate this December day.

"I am a Child of God. I am the daughter (son) of the King."

> But when the time had fully come, God sent his Son, born of a woman, born under law, to redeem those under law, that we might receive the full rights of sons. Because you are sons, God sent the Spirit of his Son into our hearts, the Spirit who calls out, "Abba, Father" (Galatians 4:4-6)

Prayer

Lord, may I never forget that I am your child. Thank you for sending Your Son, born of a woman, to redeem us and that we might receive your inheritance. And thank you that because we are sons and daughters, we can come running to You calling out "Abba, Father," and nestle under the shadow of Your wing.

The Genealogy of Jesus the Messiah

For God, who said, "Let light shine out of darkness," made His light shine in our hearts to give us the light of the knowledge of the glory of God in the face of Jesus Christ. Now we have this treasure in jars of clay to show that this surpassingly great power is from God and not from us. (2 Cor. 4:7)

During the month of December, I look forward to opening our mailbox and finding snail mail with my name and address handwritten across the front. I can't wait to catch up with dear old friends and family as they share highlights from the year.

But nobody writes about the lowlights. The marital issues, discipline problems with children, or the challenges of caring for elderly parents. Some skip greeting cards because it is not a "Holly Jolly Christmas" or "The Most Wonderful Time of the Year."

One year around Christmas time, my friend with twelve children died of a stroke, my husband's best man at our wedding passed away of ALS, my dad was diagnosed with cancer, I was temporarily working full-time, and our marital tension was at an all-time high. Not the worst on this list, but to top it all off—literally—our long-haired teenaged daughters got headlice. Not my favorite

Christmas. And, yes, all these lowlights were left out of our annual Christmas letter.

In the Bible's Christmas card to us, God shares the whole Truth. How curious that Christ's lineage is listed twice in the Christmas story (Matthew 1 and Luke 3) when most people just skim over the names. A more careful study reveals Christ's lineage includes evil kings, the prostitute Rahab, and Tamar, who bears her father-in-law's son. This patchwork of famous and infamous characters, some of whom are the result of an adulterous or illicit relationship, is also a montage of various backgrounds and religions outside the Jewish faith.

The messianic bloodline is sprinkled with those who are better candidates for the hall of shame than the hall of fame. They were NOT perfect, but through the gene pool of some very flawed individuals, God ultimately worked His perfect will.

You might not feel your annual Christmas letter measures up to Pinterest and Instagram standards, but it doesn't matter. In God's eyes, YOU measure up. And those imperfections may help others relate to you. When you are vulnerable, you connect with others who are struggling, helping them see they are not alone. When you are transparent, you form deeper, more empathetic relation-ships. You may feel like a cracked pot. But because you are broken and bruised, leaving fine fractures, fissures, and flaws, His light can shine through you.

> *Now we have this treasure in jars of clay to show that this surpassingly great power is from God and not from us. (2 Cor. 4:7)*

Need further encouragement? Those problems that threaten to bind you are nothing for the One who was not bound by death. Jesus's story includes pain and suffering. He came to earth in the most vulnerable way, then His earthly life ended with betrayal and death on a cross. And though more than a couple thousand years have passed since His birth, He is still Immanuel—God with us. For all of us who struggle, we can still claim His presence. He understands.

When some days are hard, we have marching orders and the perspective from 2 Corinthians 4:17–18 which points us to the eternal.

> *For our light and momentary troubles are achieving for us an eternal glory that far outweighs them all. So we fix our eyes not on what is seen, but on what is unseen, since what is seen is temporary, but what is unseen is eternal.*

One of my favorite Christmas "decorations" is a mini album collecting our failed attempts at Christmas photos. The pictures reveal how much work it was to get that "perfect" shot. But the imperfect ones show more character(s)! Find a photo that reminds you that we are all cracked pots and that our vulnerability may help others.

Prayer

Lord, I am an imperfect vessel. Help me to be vulnerable and admit my weaknesses. To seek counsel when needed and to share the cracks in my earthen jar. Let others see what You can do in and through me as I shine Your light. The things I go through are light and momentary in the light of eternity. May Your light shine brightly in my heart and draw others to You.

Guardian-Redeemer

> *"The LORD bless him!" Naomi said to her daughter-in-law.*
> *"He has not stopped showing his kindness to the living and*
> *the dead." She added, "That man is our close relative; he is*
> *one of our guardian-redeemers." (Ruth 2:20)*

Every other year, we travel to Seattle to spend Christmas with the Roetcisoender and/or Siemens clans. Perhaps you have a system of flipping your Christmas visits or rotating Thanksgiving and Christmas. But what if you permanently gave up your hometown, faith, and birth family for your in-laws? That's just what Ruth did.

Tucked into Matthew 1:5 is Ruth, one of the five women listed in the lineage of Christ. She has an entire Old Testament book devoted to her and it's the most beautiful and romantic in all the Bible. The book of Ruth foreshadows God's redemptive plan through Jesus Christ. In layman's terms, the story could begin, "Once upon a time, there was a widow named Ruth whom God took care of in big and small ways."

Naomi, Ruth's mother-in-law, after losing her husband and sons, determines to leave Moab to return to Bethlehem, the land of her people and faith. Ruth is loyal and caring and says, "Don't urge me to leave you or to turn back from you. Where you go I will go, and where you stay I will stay.

Your people will be my people and your God my God" (1:16). Is it no wonder her name means "friend"?

Arriving in Bethlehem, although Ruth is an outsider and foreigner, and lower than Boaz's servants, she is quickly recognized as a woman of excellence. She then meets a certain man of wealth and stature named Boaz. He just happens to be from the same family as Naomi's husband, just happens to own the field where Ruth just happens to choose to glean the leftover wheat, and just happens to possess the "finest of qualities." Boaz just happens to be a wealthy gentleman.

Do you think this just happens or was God at work in the lives of Boaz, Naomi, and Ruth for the ultimate good of His kingdom? When Boaz asks his workers to let her safely glean and to leave extra grain on the ground, he is looking out for Ruth as a protective provider. Ruth's redemption is confirmed by Boaz's ritual removal of his sandal. (You have to read the story!)

God had a wonderful future planned for Naomi and Ruth, and it wasn't just leftovers. Like Boaz, God deliberately left plenty of good grain. Similarly, we may think we're gleaning leftovers, but God is throwing much more our way than we can imagine.

The end of the story is that Ruth's obedience, love, and dedication led her to a wonderfully dear and protective man who would father a child with her in the line of David and ultimately in the lineage of Christ. By definition, a kinsman redeemer must be related by blood and must pay a price. Boaz is Ruth's Kinsman Redeemer, and Boaz foreshadows the Kinsman Redeemer who is our loving, kind, protective Jesus. You too have a Kinsman Redeemer.

Take a few unpopped kernels of corn, or a few pieces of wheat or rice, and set it out today to remind you to keep gleaning. God has a hope and a future for you. Or when you take off your shoes, let it be a reminder that YOU, too, have been redeemed.

> *He redeemed us in order that the blessing given to Abraham might come to the Gentiles through Christ Jesus, so that by faith we might receive the promise of the Spirit. Galatians 3:14*

Prayer

Jesus, nothing "just happens." You have a plan and a purpose for my life. You are my Kinsman Redeemer. Thank you for redeeming me by your blood so that, I by faith, might receive eternal life and share your redeeming love with others.

He Cares for You

*Luke 2:19 But Mary **treasured** up all these things and pondered them **in her heart**. (emphasis added)*

*Luke 2:51 But his mother **treasured** all these things **in her heart**. (emphasis added)*

By December 9th, most of the days on the December calendar are filled with events. There's the church Christmas pageant, the school winter concert, the holiday office party, your daughter's basketball games, a neighborhood dinner, and family gatherings. Between all this, you'll decorate your home, bake cookies, and buy and wrap gifts. That's the holiday schedule.

Consider Mary's schedule. Within a few months she was visited by an angel, told she was pregnant with the Son of God, and was overcome by the Holy Spirit. She broke up and reunited with her betrothed, took a lengthy trip, returned, and traveled to a foreign village while pregnant. Not only that, but she also gave birth in an unfamiliar place and was inundated by unknown visitors. That is a lot of Life Change Units or LCU's, which measure the correlation of stress on illness.[1]

Looking at Mary's changes, she had a cumulative score of over three hundred LCUs within twelve months, thus an eighty percent chance of increased illness. Consider Mary's situation as a teenage mom without a layette, crib, or the luxury of friends and family bringing her a few weeks' worth of hot meals. And yet we never hear her holler, "I'm too stressed out! Tell those smelly shepherds to go home! Joseph, is this cave the only place in town? What's the baby gonna' wear after he outgrows these swaddling clothes? Help, Mom!"

Instead, the Bible just says she pondered and treasured all these things in her heart. What was it that made her heart so capable of handling this pressure? What was the source of her peace? We get a glimpse that it might have to do with Mary's attitude. After the angel told Mary all that would happen, Mary replied, "I am the Lord's servant. May your word to me be fulfilled" (Luke 1:38). The spontaneous song she sang is one of praise for what God has done, is doing, and will do through her.

What can we learn from Mary?

Mary didn't experience a stress-free Christmas, but the Prince of Peace was there. He was all she needed, and He's still all we need for these holy days. She humbly received the words from God and rejoiced. Let's prepare our hearts with prayer and study so that despite the Life Change Units of the holidays, we treasure and ponder the wonder of our Savior.

Today, let's have a "Mary little Christmas." Pour a cup of hot tea, open your Bible, and find a quiet place to ponder and treasure. Enjoy reading Mary's Song aloud.

Lord, I am your servant. Help me ponder and treasure all that your Word tells us about you. When I become stressed out, let me cast my anxiety on you because you care for me (1 Peter 5:7). Help me press "pause" in the middle of a busy day and listen to you. As I pause in your presence, remind me that I am your child and You are Wonderful Counselor and Prince of Peace.

Mary's Song (Luke 1:46–55)

And Mary said:

"My soul glorifies the Lord
and my spirit rejoices in God my Savior,
for he has been mindful of the humble state of his servant.

From now on all generations will call me blessed,
for the Mighty One has done great things for me—holy is his name.

His mercy extends to those who fear him,
  from generation to generation.
He has performed mighty deeds with his arm;
  he has scattered those who are proud in their inmost thoughts.

He has brought down rulers from their thrones
   but has lifted up the humble.
He has filled the hungry with good things
   but has sent the rich away empty.
He has helped his servant Israel,
   remembering to be merciful
to Abraham and his descendants forever,
   just as he promised our ancestors."

Think about Such Things

> "You are worthy, our Lord and God, to receive glory and
> honor and power, for you created all things, and by your will
> they were created and have their being." (Revelation 4:11)

When I first watched the Christmas movie *The Polar Express*, I was struck by the fantastic moment when Santa appears to the crowd amidst great awe and adulation by the people below. I couldn't help but imagine how much greater the moment will be when we see Jesus and the angels proclaim, "Holy, Holy, Holy is the Lord God Almighty, who was, and is, and is to come" (Revelation 4:8).

Like *The Polar Express*, so many of our family favorites have a moral, a takeaway truth that can be appreciated and discussed after watching.

Annabelle's Wish tells a tale of a boy named Billy who lost his voice after witnessing a tragedy. His grandfather gave him a calf named Annabelle, born on Christmas Eve, a day when Santa has gifted all the animals with the ability to talk. Annabelle's secret wish is to fly like a reindeer, and so she determines to ask Santa to grant her that wish. But when Christmas Eve arrives, instead she sacrifices her ability to talk, and her wish to fly so that Billy has the gift of speech.

Another holiday favorite with a spiritual takeaway is Dickens's *A Christmas Carol.* Ebenezer Scrooge encourages me. Once he repents, he wastes not a minute wallowing in guilt over his PAST. He doesn't focus on his prior cruelty, regretting where his choices have taken him, and feeling depressed over his age and circumstances in the PRESENT. Instead, he is able to forgive himself and make a change for the FUTURE. He is a fictional example of Psalm 32:1: "Blessed is the one whose transgressions are forgiven, whose sins are covered."

Scrooge determines to spend the rest of his days doing good. He generously bestows his love, finances, and attention on all those he meets. And how does that make him feel?

"I am as light as a feather, I am as happy as an angel, I am as merry as a schoolboy!" And he shouts, "MERRY CHRISTMAS!" to the world.

He reminds me of what the Lord offers, "Though your sins are like scarlet, they shall be as white as snow; though they are red as crimson, they shall be like wool" (Isaiah 1:18).

Family classics bring us together, and if they're worth enjoying together, they're worth taking the time to discuss together.

How are God's truths illustrated?

Is there a moral to this story?

What can I learn about what is true, noble, and right?

We are encouraged by Paul to do just that.

> *Finally, brothers and sisters, whatever is true, whatever is noble, whatever is right, whatever is pure, whatever is lovely, whatever is admirable—if anything is excellent or praiseworthy—think about such things. (Philippians 4:8)*

WHATEVER! is a word we sometimes use in desperation, but it can also be used to remind us to think about WHATEVER is....

True
Noble
Right
Pure
Lovely
Admirable
Excellent
Praiseworthy

That list, or even the word WHATEVER! is a great visual reminder to put near your TV to prompt discussion.

Prayer

Lord, this Christmas season may I focus on what is true and lovely. May I look for forgiveness, reconciliation, and redemption in the stories I see and remember the greatest story of all eternity is about you. Prompt me to remember WHATEVER to think and talk about.

All Is Bright: A Great Light

the people living in darkness
  have seen a great light;
on those living in the land of the shadow of death
  a light has dawned." Matthew 4:16

During the holiday season, Christmas lights outline rooftops and windows, they encircle evergreens and illuminate front yards. Luminaries light up the walkways, a roaring fireplace brings a warm glow to the home, decorative lanterns, and fireworks cheer the darkness.

I especially enjoy seeing single candle lights twinkling in windows to welcome me home. How appropriate that at Christmas we celebrate with lights the birthday of the one who is the Light of the World.

The people of old sat in darkness waiting for their Savior. Zechariah tells us God sent His Son "to shine on those living in darkness and in the shadow of death, to guide our feet into the path of peace" (Luke 1:79).

How beautiful. Jesus makes it clear that He is that light shining in darkness to guide our feet into the path of peace when He says, "I have come into the world as a light, so that no one who believes in me should stay in darkness" (John 12:46) and "I am the light of the world. Whoever follows me will never walk in darkness but will have the light of life" (John 8:12).

But the light doesn't stop there. Jesus says WE are to be lights.

> "You are the light of the world. A town built on a hill cannot be hidden. (Matthew 5:14)

> "In the same way, let your light shine before others, that they may see your good deeds and glorify your Father in heaven. (Matthew 5:16)

Our light shines through good deeds that glorify God! And when we walk in the light, we have fellowship with others.

> But if we walk in the light, as he is in the light, we have fellowship with one another, and the blood of Jesus, his Son, purifies us from all sin. (1 John 1:7)

Did you know that you can see a candle flame from almost two miles away? Though it's not a Christmas song, maybe we should all sing, "This little light of mine, I'm gonna let it shine!"

Prayer

Lord, Sometimes the world seems so dark. I am so glad I have You as the Light of my life. I want to be a light for You. Let Your light shine through me out of darkness. Keep me in fellowship with other believers and looking to Your Word for light to do good deeds that glorify You.

Joseph, Son of David

But after he had considered this, an angel of the Lord appeared to him in a dream and said, "Joseph son of David, do not be afraid to take Mary home as your wife, because what is conceived in her is from the Holy Spirit. She will give birth to a son, and you are to give him the name Jesus, because he will save his people from their sins." When Joseph woke up, he did what the angel of the Lord had commanded him and took Mary home as his wife. (Matthew 1:20-21)

I remember how I worried when leaving my young kids home with a babysitter. I wonder what it took for God to hand over His only Son to an imperfect earthly father. What qualities was God looking for in this adoptive dad? And what was it like for Joseph to consider raising God's perfect Son as His own?

"Joseph's Prayer" from *The Nativity Alive* asks just that.

I am just a lowly carpenter, why would you choose me?
To be the earthly father for your only Son.
God help me to be the kind of father that You are to me.
Loving, gentle, and full of wisdom.
Lord this is my plea. God help me to see.

Joseph may be the most unassuming character in the Nativity. But he's one of my favorites.

If Joseph followed Jewish tradition, he would have researched Mary's parentage, ancestry, and resources, and traced the line of David. He would then have asked her parents if Mary could be his wife. Both sets would have had to agree.

At the betrothal ceremony, Joseph and Mary sipped from a shared cup of wine, finalizing their legal betrothal. If Joseph died, Mary would have been considered a widow. This sacred engagement was basically marriage without living together or consummation. The wedding would come next, but instead Joseph learned of Mary's pregnancy, which must have caused disappointment and quite a dilemma for Jesus' earthly dad.

Thankfully, Joseph listens to his heavenly Father whenever he is told what to do, where to go, and when to leave. We never hear Joseph question God about His instructions or doubt the plans God gives him to protect the family.

Luke 2 doesn't tell us Joseph became frustrated and anxious when rooms in Bethlehem at tax time were at a premium. After all, didn't Joseph have the right to yell, "My wife is in labor and she's going to have a really SPECIAL baby!" Instead, he was at peace, recognizing that Immanuel, God with us, would soon be with them.

His attitude makes me wonder how he came to such maturity. I'm curious about how and what Joseph's parents taught him. Perhaps they followed these Old Testament instructions on how to teach.

> "<u>These commandments</u> that I give you today are to be upon your hearts. Impress them on your children. Talk about them when you sit at home and when you walk along the road, when you lie down and when you get up. Tie them as symbols on your hands and bind them on your foreheads. Write them on the door frames of your houses and on your gates" (Deuteronomy 6:6-9).

What are "<u>these commandments</u>" to be written down? What are the words so precious that Jesus will remind us of them in the New Testament as well? Glad you asked!

> "Hear, O Israel: The Lord is our God, the Lord is one. Love the Lord your God with all your heart and with all your soul and with all your strength." (Deuteronomy 6:4-5)

Unassuming, loving, serving, and obedient Joseph sets a positive example for all of us. What the Lord asked of Israel is still pertinent today, "to fear the Lord your God, to walk in obedience to him, to serve the Lord your God with all your heart and with all your soul. (Deuteronomy 10:12)

Jesus reinforces those words in the New Testament when asked "What is the greatest commandment.

"*Love the Lord your God with all your heart and with all your soul and with all your mind and with all your strength.* The second is this: 'Love your neighbor as yourself. There is no commandment greater than these." (Mark 12:28–31)

Where can you write the words underlined above on *your* door frame or gates?

Prayer

Lord, just as Joseph knew the Word and the God of Israel, I want to study the Bible and learn to walk in obedience. I want to be the kind of person that inspires a believer to know You and Your Word. I want to sit and walk and talk about Your Word, always bearing testimony of my faith. Please help me love and serve You with wholehearted devotion.

Bethlehem: Though You Are Small

*"But you, **Bethlehem** Ephrathah,*
though you are small among the clans of Judah,
out of you will come for me
one who will be ruler over Israel,
whose origins are from of old, from ancient times." Micah 5:2

So Joseph also went up from the town of Nazareth in Galilee
*to Judea, to **Bethlehem** the town of David, because he*
belonged to the house and line of David. (Luke 2:4)

"Does not Scripture say that the Messiah will come from
*David's descendants and from **Bethlehem**, the town*
where David lived?" John 7:42

Though you are small, O Little Town of Bethlehem, you are a BIG deal.

In Bethlehem, the House of Bread, Ruth gleaned wheat and was blessed with a Kinsman Redeemer. On the way to Bethlehem, Rachel was laid to rest. King David the shepherd king was born, foreshadowing the birth of another Shepherd King —the one called Prince of Peace and Bread of Life; the one who is our Kinsman Redeemer.

Bethlehem has quite a history, and it is here that "the hopes and fears of all the years are met in thee tonight."

Perhaps no one understood this better than Pastor Phillip Brooks, the lyricist for "O Little Town of Bethlehem." After President Lincoln's assassination, he was asked to deliver the funeral message. Brooks, an abolitionist, was worn out and discouraged with the Civil War. Needing a time for rest and reflection, Brooks took a sabbatical tour to the Middle East.

On that Christmas Eve in 1865, Brooks stood in the shepherds' field outside the little town of Bethlehem. As stars twinkled overhead, he experienced an overwhelming feeling of being present at the very first Christmas. Though greatly moved by the emotion of his experience for many years, Brooks was unable to convey the experience to his congregation. After he wrote the words, his organist struggled to set the lyrics to music, until Christmas Day, when he awoke with the melody and harmony in his head, calling it a "gift from heaven."[2]

O little town of Bethlehem,
How still we see thee lie!
Above thy deep and dreamless sleep
The silent stars go by;
Yet in the dark street shineth
The everlasting Light;
The hopes and fears of all the years
Are met in thee tonight.

For Christ is born of Mary,
And gathered all above,
While mortals sleep, the angels keep
Their watch of wondering love.
O morning stars, together
Proclaim the holy birth
And praises sing to God, the King,
And peace to men on earth.

How silently, how silently,
The wondrous Gift is given!
So God imparts to human hearts
The blessings of His heaven.
No ear may hear His coming,
But in this world of sin,
Where meek souls will receive Him still,
The dear Christ enters in.

O holy Child of Bethlehem,
Descend to us, we pray;
Cast out our sin and enter in,
Be born in us today.
We hear the Christmas angels
The great glad tidings tell:
Oh, come to us, abide with us,
*Our Lord **Immanuel**!*

Indeed, what a gift from heaven! If you've never allowed the Lord to be born in your heart, there is no time like today. Christ will come and abide, for He is Immanuel—God with us.

> *"When the angels had left them and gone into heaven, the shepherds said to one another, 'Let's go to **Bethlehem** and see this thing that has happened, which the Lord has told us about.'" (Luke 2:15)*

Maybe we can't all go to Bethlehem for Christmas, but perhaps there is a part of us that can close our eyes and be there. Each time you hear "O Little Town of Bethlehem," put yourself there under the stars, seeing the shepherds and the angels, and the Magi and most of all, the One who meets all the hopes and fears of all the years.

Prayer

Lord, cast out my sin and enter in with the blessings of heaven. I receive You Jesus. Impart the blessings of your heaven. Be born in my heart today. Abide with me, always, Immanuel.

Your Prayer Has Been Heard

*But the angel said to him: "Do not be afraid, Zechariah;
your prayer has been heard. Your wife Elizabeth will bear
you a son, and you are to call him John. He will be a joy and
delight to you, and many will rejoice because of his birth
(Luke 1:13-14)*

Have you ever had a once-in-a-lifetime experience? Met
the President, viewed a comet, or celebrated your only
child's first birthday?

Elderly Zechariah, a priest, traveled to the temple to offer
sacrifice and prayers ONCE in his lifetime. "Coincidentally"
that ONE time would become unforgettable.

He probably spent the night sleeping near the temple,
anticipating the next day's entrance into the sacred place
where he would meet with the Most Holy God.[3]

He entered the Holy of Holies to burn incense, and he
also offered his prayers for the nation of Israel, and for
a Messiah. And perhaps he had a secret prayer on the
side—one that was quite an impossibility. Though he and
his wife are described as righteous and a couple who obey
all God's commands, they are elderly and childless. Why
Zechariah and Elizabeth had been denied a child into their
old age was unclear. But in their time, many considered

childlessness a curse from God, believing their status was God's punishment.

Even today, is it ever clear why a wonderful couple is unable to conceive? The empty void is accompanied by the painful question, "Why can't we have a baby?"

God had a reason Zechariah would not be able to fathom. Zechariah couldn't know God's timing and bigger picture and that his family name would be more than carried on!

Suddenly, while in the temple, an angel appeared to him. The angel knew Zechariah's secret prayer and promised that in their old age, Elizabeth would bear a son.

Timing is everything. Like Abraham and Sarah, can you imagine how God might have longed to give Zechariah and Elizabeth the whole picture during the decades they, too, prayed for a child? "Zechariah, you will have a child. A child that will prepare the way for the Messiah! The one prophesied in Isaiah seven hundred years before as the voice of one crying in the wilderness: "Prepare ye the way of the Lord." The one who is the messenger (Malachi 3:1) and the very one prophesied as the Elijah to come in the very last verses of the Old Testament.

> *Behold, I will send you Elijah the prophet before the coming of the great and awesome Day of the LORD. And he will turn the hearts of the fathers to their children, and the hearts of the children to their fathers. (Malachi 4:5-6)*

What glorious "YES" news that would have been for Zechariah years earlier!

Sometimes God says "Yes"; sometimes, "No"; and sometimes, "Wait." But in one momentous encounter, God answered Zechariah's prayers of the past and present, as well as the prayers of thousands of Jews for many centuries. And even as the angel proclaimed the "Yes," we know that Zechariah could not fathom the good news.

> *And he will go on before the Lord, in the spirit and power of Elijah, to turn the hearts of the parents to their children and the disobedient to the wisdom of the righteous—to make ready a people prepared for the Lord. (Luke 1:17)*

In today's prayer, go ahead and fill in the blanks. He hears you.

Prayer

Dear Lord, I know you have heard my secret prayers. The Holy Spirit understands my groanings even when I cannot utter the words. You know how to fill in the blanks and empty spaces in my life. You know that I have been praying for_____. You know how I need _____ and you know the right timing. I thank you for past answers to prayer _____ and how you are at work in my present situation with _____ and I thank you for future answered prayer. I know that you will answer my prayers with yes, no, or wait. May I rest in your peace as I wait for your timing and will.

And Now You Will Be Silent

> *Zechariah asked the angel, "How can I be sure of this? I am an old man and my wife is well along in years." The angel said to him, "I am Gabriel. I stand in the presence of God, and I have been sent to speak to you and to tell you this good news. And now you will be silent and not able to speak until the day this happens, because you did not believe my words, which will come true at their appointed time." (Luke 1:18-20)*

One December, my speech therapist ordered me to go on vocal rest for a month from December 10 through January 7. "Impossible!" I told her. "I have to direct four Christmas pageants this week, and I'm going home to Seattle for the holidays to catch up with friends and family I haven't seen for a year! She responded by writing me a list: no talking, no coughing, no laughing. She might as well have put me in a dark room with white noise. For me, the holidays were over. That Christmas I held a sign in front of me: ZECHARIAH.

It always got a laugh. But during that December, I began to understand his pain. Communication was slow and clunky with hand motions and hastily scribbled notes. My friends unknowingly imitated me, forgetting they could talk.

Which, ironically, is what Zechariah's friends did as well! "Then they made signs to his father, to find out what he would like to name the child." (Luke 1:62)

My husband became the interpreter, and I became the listener, a frustrating identity change. I never realized how much I used my voice until I tried to direct a show, corral my kids, or greet friends at a Christmas gathering.

Zechariah had it a lot worse. When he doubted the angel's words as he served in the temple, he couldn't talk for nine months. When Zechariah came home from the temple, just what kind of signs would he make to his wife to convey an angelic appearance telling him that the Messiah was coming, and his wife would bear a son? I would love to have seen that discussion! This must have changed his capacity to serve as a priest. He must have been frustrated.

And I wonder what his silence taught him.

My husband considered my prescribed silence as a gift. No, it is not because I talk too much! The inability to speak made me a more sensitive listener. Quiet people were suddenly comfortable around a less outgoing me. As I listened, I really heard what people said.

Over the holidays we hear brass music and Christmas carols; we listen to bells ringing, and we cherish the laughter of children. The sounds of the season are a gift, opened with our ears. During this time, are we quiet enough to hear God singing over us? Listen and learn what the Lord of love has to say.

> *"The Lord your God is with you, he is mighty to save. He will take great delight in you, he will quiet you with his love, he will rejoice over you with singing. (Zephaniah 3:17)*

Prayer

Dear God, help me appreciate the gift of hearing. I thank you for music and laughter and the sound of quiet. May I listen to you singing over me. May I hear what you want me to hear and attend to your voice in all I do. Help me pay attention to the stories of others and take heed to their needs.

Nothing Is Impossible for God!

The angel answered, "The Holy Spirit will come down to you, and God's power will come over you. So your child will be called the holy Son of God. Your relative Elizabeth is also going to have a son, even though she is old. No one thought she could ever have a baby, but in three months she will have a son. Nothing is impossible for God!"

Mary said, "I am the Lord's servant! Let it happen as you have said." And the angel left her. (Luke 1:35–38 CEV)

When the angel told the teenaged virgin Mary she would conceive and bear a son and this child would be the long-awaited Messiah, Mary must have been overwhelmed. After all, this was an impossible scenario; Mary had not consummated her relationship with Joseph.

The King James Version reads, "She was troubled at his saying, and cast in her mind what manner of salutation this should be" (Luke 1:29).

Mary's one question "How will this be, since I am a virgin?" (v. 34) is not one of doubt, but of puzzlement. The angel's response is for all of us. "Nothing is impossible for God" (CEV). Mary heard the words, believed, and responded with humility, "I am the Lord's servant. May it be to me as you have said."

With God, the impossible becomes possible. He parts the Red Sea, drops manna from heaven, brings water from a rock, crumbles the walls of Jericho, shields three men in the fiery furnace and Daniel in a den of lions, calls upon a whale to rescue Jonah, and fires up a bush to burn without being consumed.

> *"Ah, Sovereign Lord, you have made the heavens and the earth by your great power and outstretched arm. Nothing is too hard for you." (Jeremiah 32:17)*

I don't know what's going on in your life this December, but nothing is impossible for God. Your journey may be quite different than Mary's; and yet, nothing is impossible for God. Not then, and certainly not now.

When I teach my students how to do cold reads for theatre auditions, I ask them to find the most important words in their script and underline them. This can involve trying out all the words in the sentence to discover all the potential meanings. If you take Luke 1:37 and read it, emphasizing a different word each time, you'll experience the fullness of its meaning.

NOTHING is impossible for God.
Nothing IS impossible for God.
Nothing is IMPOSSIBLE for God.
Nothing is impossible FOR God.
Nothing is impossible for GOD.

By emphasizing each word separately, you realize that even when you're weak, He is strong.

Knowing nothing is impossible for God, what can you look forward to next year? What are you waiting to do that can be accomplished with His help? Today, claim, "Nothing is impossible for God" in writing or in song. Shout these words aloud as you go throughout your day or post them in big letters on your refrigerator.

> *"My grace is sufficient for you, for my power is made perfect in weakness." Therefore I will boast all the more gladly about my weaknesses, so that Christ's power may rest on me." (2 Corinthians 12:9)*

Prayer

Lord, you know what's going on in my life. Sometimes it feels like there's a stone too big to roll away. But then I remember Your message delivered through the angel. Nothing is impossible for God. And I know, Lord, that the message is for me, too. Your power is perfected in my weakness. You rolled the gravestone away. Help me accomplish all that You have set before me.

A New Song

He put a new song in my mouth, a hymn of praise to our God. Many will see and fear the Lord and put their trust in him. (Psalm 40:3)

My close friend Carolyn announced she was pregnant, and the next week I discovered I was also pregnant. We commiserated about nausea, shopped for baby supplies, and predicted the sexes of our children (with 50% chance of accuracy, we were both 100% wrong). Sharing the excitement doubled our anticipation. Our December babies were gifts with a lot of presence!

Can you imagine how Mary hungered to share her experience and the secret news with her older relative, Elizabeth, and also soon-to-be a first-time mom? And yet look at their differences. Mary was expecting much earlier than she planned, and Elizabeth far later. Mary was expecting but was not married. Elizabeth had been married for decades with no offspring.

How comforting for Mary to have an older and wiser woman who was also a part of this amazing plan. Though Mary's hasty departure for Elizabeth's home in the hill country included no quick telephone call, text, e-mail, and probably not even a letter, Elizabeth miraculously knew Mary's status.

In a loud voice she exclaimed;

> *"Blessed are you among women, and blessed is the child
> you will bear! But why am I so favored, that the mother of
> my Lord should come to me? As soon as the sound of your
> greeting reached my ears, the baby in my womb leaped for
> joy. Blessed is she who has believed that what the Lord has
> said to her will be accomplished!" (Luke 1:42-45)*

We almost expect Mary to say, "But Aunt Elizabeth, how could you know? It's as if Mary and Elizabeth are two halves of a heart locket, holding secrets the world cannot yet fathom.

After Elizabeth's greeting, Mary spontaneously rejoices, "My soul glorifies the Lord and my spirit rejoices in God my Savior," (Luke 1:46) and goes into a song of praise based on a thorough knowledge of scripture, a heart of thanksgiving, and recognition of God's mercy (Luke 1:46–55).

Similarly, when Zechariah's mouth is opened to sing, he too praises God for who He is, what He is doing, and what He will do. He describes Jesus as a horn of salvation, the symbol of light, and a guide for our feet. (v. 78)

What spills out of our hearts and mouths this Christmas? Did you know that the phrase "new song" is listed nine times in the Bible? We are encouraged to sing a new song!

Prayer

Today your prayer is to write out a song or lift your voice in a new song to God. Read Zechariah's song of praise for inspiration!

Zechariah's Song

67 His father Zechariah was filled with the Holy Spirit and prophesied:

68 "Praise be to the Lord, the God of Israel,
because he has come to his people and redeemed them.

69 He has raised up a horn of salvation for us
in the house of his servant David

70 (as he said through his holy prophets of long ago),

71 salvation from our enemies
and from the hand of all who hate us—

72 to show mercy to our ancestors
and to remember his holy covenant,

73 the oath he swore to our father Abraham:

74 to rescue us from the hand of our enemies,
and to enable us to serve him without fear

75 in holiness and righteousness before him all our days.

76 And you, my child, will be called a prophet of the Most High;
for you will go on before the Lord to prepare the way for him,

77 to give his people the knowledge of salvation
   through the forgiveness of their sins,
78 because of the tender mercy of our God,
   by which the rising sun will come to us from heaven
79 to shine on those living in darkness
   and in the shadow of death,
to guide our feet into the path of peace." (Luke 1:67–79)

His Own Did Not Receive Him

When they had seen him, they spread the word concerning what had been told them about this child (Luke 2:17)

One Christmas, we planned to fly from Virginia to Washington State. The night before we left, the temperature dropped, and it began to snow. As I began washing clothes for the trip, I discovered the pipes were frozen. So stressed out that we'd leave and then return to a flooded house, I proposed we should just stay home. I assumed our Christmas canceled.

The snow continued falling in big, beautiful flakes, and so my husband took our two-year-old daughter outside to let the snowflakes fall on her face. She delighted in her winter surprise. But as I filled baskets with dirty laundry, and crammed packages in suitcases, my indoor song was one of whining, fear, and grumbling.

A gracious neighbor not only washed, but also folded my laundry. We left for Washington with pipes still frozen. Guess what? They never broke. But by refusing to receive the joy of that snowy day, I missed my toddler's first taste of snow. That still makes me sad. I missed a big first.

It makes me wonder about Bethlehem villagers during tax season. Jesus was in their midst. Did they notice a baby was born? Some townsfolk might have spotted two ragged travelers entering a crowded village. Some may have seen only a poor family in a cave and a baby in a manger. Some may have been annoyed with ecstatic shepherds with a story to tell. The Bible is silent about their reactions.

What would have happened if the shepherds hadn't left their sheep? If they doubted the angels or said their job was more important? What if the wisemen thought the journey too far and involved? What if they were distracted from coming to the manger?

What might distract us from focusing on Jesus this season? Work? Worry? School? Obligations? Unrealistic expectations for the holidays? Church activities? Shopping lists and lines?

It wasn't just at His birth that people might have missed Him. They didn't recognize Him later in His adult ministry, especially in Nazareth.

> *He was in the world, and though the world was made through him, the world did not recognize him. He came to that which was his own, but his own did not receive him. (John 1:10-11)*

Let's make sure *we* recognize Him. That we remember our first love and the way it felt when we first met Him. Can we go back to the beginning and with a childlike faith see the baby, the angels, and the shepherds and remember how much God must love us to send His only Son? Shut your eyes to distractions, close out the noise and think back to a time when you experienced childlike wonder. Let the "snow" fall on your face.

Now think back to the first time you met Jesus. He is still with you.

Jesus was there during Bethlehem's chaos, and thank God He is here today in the busyness of ours. Jesus is Immanuel, God with us.

> *Now this is eternal life: that they know you, the only true God, and Jesus Christ, whom you have sent. (John 17:3)*

Prayer

Lord help me not to miss you in this Advent season. Let me not be distracted by business and busyness but instead looking for You in all that I say and do. I want to recognize and receive You. I want to know You, the only true God and Jesus Christ, whom You have sent so that I would know You better.

The Good Shepherd

> *"I am the good shepherd; I know my sheep and my sheep know me—just as the Father knows me and I know the Father—and I lay down my life for the sheep" (John 10:14–15).*

With two-dozen sheep running around our backyard, I have new insight into pastoral passages from the Bible about shepherds and sheep, and though I hate to admit it, being compared with sheep is not exactly a compliment.

Sheep get lost easily; they are defenseless, and their worst predator is the domestic dog, which can chase them silly. If they fall over, they are sometimes unable, or unwilling, to get back up. You've heard of "cow-tipping," but probably not "sheep-tipping." When I find a ewe flipped over in the field or "downcast," she has given up and no longer can get up. I have to right her myself. Interestingly, the term "downcast" is used throughout the Bible in a comparable way.

> *"Why, my soul, are you **downcast**? Why so disturbed within me? Put your hope in God, for I will yet praise him, my Savior and my God." (Psalm 42:11)*

Who took care of these helpless animals surrounding Bethlehem? Lowly, young shepherds with minimal education and spiritual knowledge. The shepherds endured harsh weather in primitive wild lodgings and defended themselves against animals, lions, bears, wolves, and thieves, while protecting animals they didn't own.

Clothed in heavy cloaks, carrying staffs and rods, their familiar presence and voices were a reassurance to their flocks as they cared for expectant ewes, newborn lambs, and sick animals. At night, as the sheep entered their enclosures, the shepherds counted them with their rods and then became a gate by sleeping at the entrance to protect them.[4]

Who could imagine that lowly *shepherds* would be the first to hear the good news? The night Jesus was born, an angel revealed it to the least likely to receive a royal pronouncement. Philip Yancey writes:

> For just an instant the sky grew luminous with angels, yet who saw that spectacle? Illiterate hirelings who watched the flocks of others, "nobodies" who failed to leave their names. Shepherds had such a randy reputation that proper Jews lumped them together with the "godless," restricting them to the outer court-yards of the temple. Fittingly, it was they whom God selected to help celebrate the birth of one who would be known as the friend of sinners.[5]

The "friend of sinners" is Jesus. He is a friend of sinners who will save his people from their sins. The announcement is for all of us. We are all sinners in need of a Savior.

He is our Good Shepherd who will encourage the downcast. "He tends his flock like a shepherd: He gathers the lambs in his arms and carries them close to his heart; he gently leads those that have young" (Isaiah 40:11). What a beautiful picture to meditate on.

Prayer

Picture being cradled by the Good Shepherd. Today we'll pray the 23rd Psalm to close.

> *The Lord is my shepherd, I lack nothing.*
> *2 He makes me lie down in green pastures,*
> *he leads me beside quiet waters,*
> *3 he refreshes my soul.*
> *He guides me along the right paths*
> *   for his name's sake.*
> *4 Even though I walk*
> *   through the darkest valley,*
> *I will fear no evil,*
> *   for you are with me;*
> *your rod and your staff,*
> *   they comfort me.*

5 *You prepare a table before me*
   in the presence of my enemies.
You anoint my head with oil;
   my cup overflows.
6 *Surely your goodness and love will follow me*
   all the days of my life,
and I will dwell in the house of the LORD
   forever.

Good News!

And there were shepherds living out in the fields nearby, keeping watch over their flocks at night. An angel of the Lord appeared to them, and the glory of the Lord shone around them, and they were terrified. (Luke 10:8-9)

One of the best sentences in the entire Christmas story appears in the very next verse (v. 10).

But the angel said to them, "Do not be afraid. I bring you good news that will cause great joy for all the people."

This sentence has four amazing parts. Let's break it down.

Do not be afraid. Something about angels must elicit fear. What exactly did Zechariah, Mary, Joseph, and the shepherds see? Probably not first graders in white robes with silver halos being told by their parents not to be afraid. Was it the wings of seraphim and cherubim? The only angelic description we have is that the angel was accompanied by the glory of the Lord. Nevertheless, who wouldn't want to hear the angel's words of assurance?

I bring you good news. When someone says that, I can hardly wait! But this good news will literally change their world, their lives, and their future.

Great Joy. Now I'm really listening. JOY is wonderful, and we all want it!

For all the people. That's me!

We are **all the people,** and we have been given **good news** and **great joy**, and we are to **fear not**!

Nothing about that angelic message has changed. We don't have to be afraid because we, too, have the Good News of Jesus Christ, and it elicits Great Joy for all people. Can you even comprehend what it sounded like coming from an angel?

I love singing "Angels We Have Heard on High" Because of its meandering, eighteen-note melisma on the word Gloria! This song makes anyone sound great even without the echoing chamber of a shower stall! What words of praise! "Glory to God in the highest!" or Gloria ("glory") in excelsis ("in the highest") Deo ("God").

The first verse of "Angels We Have Heard on High" tells of Jesus' birth from the shepherds' perspective; the second from perhaps a curious Bethlehem resident asking about the shepherds' joyous jubilee. "Say what may the tidings be, which inspire your heavenly song?" The third is the shepherds' answer, inviting others—or perhaps all of us—to "Come to Bethlehem and see, Him whose birth the angels sing; Come adore on bended knee, Christ the Lord, the newborn King." And finally, we arrive and "see within a manger laid" the one who is Lord not only of earth but also of heaven.

We, too, are nearing the cradle. Like the angels and the shepherds who rejoice at the newborn King, our joy will be full. So full, we, like these messengers, can deliver the Good News to others. From wherever you are, go to bended knee and adore Him, reading:

> *Suddenly a great company of the heavenly host appeared*
> *with the angel, praising God and saying,*
> *"Glory to God in the highest heaven,*
> *and on earth peace to those on whom his favor rests."*
> *(Luke 2:13-14)*

Angels we have on heard high
Sweetly singing o'er the plains
And the mountains in reply
Echoing their joyous strains

Come to Bethlehem and see
Christ whose birth the angels sing
Come adore on bended knee
Christ the Lord the newborn King

See him in a manger laid
Whom the choirs of angels praise

Mary, Joseph, lend your aid
While our hearts in love we raise

Prayer

Lord, let me never forget that this verse is for me, too. The good news of the gospel has been given to me, and it brings great joy to me. But it's not only for me. So, like the shepherds, help me hurry to share that joy so others might enjoy the good news and glorify you.

And She Gave Birth

> *"In those days Caesar Augustus issued a decree that a census should be taken of the entire Roman world. (This was the first census that took place while Quirinius was governor of Syria.) And everyone went to their own town to register.*
>
> *So Joseph also went up from the town of Nazareth in Galilee to Judea, to Bethlehem the town of David, because he belonged to the house and line of David. He went there to register with Mary, who was pledged to be married to him and was expecting a child." (Luke 2:1-5)*

I remember the fantastic story of one surprise delivery near our local airport.

While traveling from New York to Florida prior to Christmas, a seven-month pregnant woman went into early delivery at thirty thousand feet. Flight attendants flew into action rounding up linens and blankets, calling play by play and asking for a doctor. The internist on board hadn't delivered a baby in thirteen years, and when the mother began hemorrhaging, it forced an emergency landing.

As the baby emerged, a cord was wrapped around the neck, and it was blue and not breathing. Dulles Airport was still ninety miles away. Two paramedics onboard, experienced in infant respiratory procedure, requested a straw to suction fluid from the newborn's lungs. None could be found until a flight attendant remembered her juice box with the bendable straw. A passenger contributed a shoelace to tie off the umbilical cord. Meanwhile, the mother prayed as the straw was placed down her newborn's throat and CPR begun. Suddenly the infant was breathing! The flight attendant announced, "It's a boy!" to the relief and applause of the 150 passengers on board.

His place of birth is: IN FLIGHT and his parents toyed with naming their 4-pound, 6-ounce baby, "747, or "TWA." But because medical personnel had dubbed him Dulles after the airport where he landed, the couple settled on *Matthew Dulles*, meaning gift from God, recognizing it as a "midair miracle."[6] And when Matthew Dulles asks about the day he was born, it will make a great story.

I wonder if Jesus ever asked Mary and Joseph about the night of His birth? The premise for the pageant "Happy Birthday, Jesus" is that twelve-year-old Jesus asks his mother Mary about the night he was born.

Perhaps Mary's answer began, "Well, Jesus, the trip to Bethlehem was eighty miles, and it took five days...."
Did she tell him they traveled past the Mount of Olives and Gethsemane? Would he have comprehended their

magnitude regarding the end of his life? Did she tell Jesus about the significance of Bethlehem, the prophecy, and Ruth and Boaz, and King David?

"Well, Jesus, you were born in a small village that was very crowded because everybody came to pay their taxes." Mary might have paused then. How much should she tell of the dark and dirty caves dotting the hills around the village? The soot-stained ceiling, the layers of caked manure on a floor not recently mucked. About how they looked for where she could deliver him and what kind of bed they could fashion?[7]

What came next? Who delivered the Son of God? Mid-wives usually assisted in delivering, and husbands were not allowed to help. Did she tell him about the swaddling clothes and the feeding trough?

But for all of us who celebrate the humble birth of the King of Kings, Christmas would not mean anything without celebrating His life, death, and resurrection. Because of all of that, we can celebrate His birthday and re-tell and re-enact the story every year.

You have a story about the day you were born or gave birth, or a friend's delivery drama. Ask any mother about a birth day and you'll get a good story! It's a conversation starter with whomever you meet and a way to share about the humble birth of our Savior.

While they were there, the time came for the baby to be born, and she gave birth to her firstborn, a son. She wrapped him in cloths and placed him in a manger, because there was no guest room available for them. (Luke 2:67)

> *"This will be a sign to you: You will find a baby wrapped in cloths and lying in a manger." (Luke 2:12)*

Prayer

Jesus, I will never tire of this story. May I read it every Christmas and hold it close to my heart all year long as I celebrate and follow your life. At Easter, when we celebrate Your death and resurrection, may I grasp more fully not just your earthly life but our future heavenly one with You.

Let's Go to Bethlehem!

*Today in the town of David a Savior has been born to you;
he is the Messiah, the Lord. (Luke 2:11 emphasis added)*

"Run, Run, Run to the Stable" was the title of the shepherd's song in Come to the Manger.

*"We'll run, run, run 'til we find Him
We'll search, search, search 'til He's heard.
We'll run through the night to see the glorious sight
of the Living Promise of God's Word."*

Any one of the titles: Savior, Messiah, Lord would be a great reason to RUN to Bethlehem. Which is exactly what the shepherds do. They are full of action. The verbs are underlined below.

> *When the angels had left them and gone into heaven, the shepherds said to one another, "Let's <u>go</u> to Bethlehem and <u>see</u> this thing that has happened, which the Lord has told us about."*

> *So they <u>hurried</u> off and <u>found</u> Mary and Joseph, and the baby, who was lying in the manger. When they had <u>seen</u> him, they <u>spread</u> the word concerning what had been told them about this child, (Luke 2:8, 15-17)*

Their actions don't stop there.

> *The shepherds returned, glorifying and praising God for all*
> *the things they had heard and seen, which were just as they*
> *had been told. (Luke 2:20)*

"Let's Go and See!"
"Let's Hurry!"
"Let's Find!"
"Let's Spread the word."
"Let's Glorify and Praise God!"

Now the big question: What do *we* do with the story of Jesus' birth? What do *we* do with the *Good News of Great Joy for All People*? Can we be more like the shepherds? This year, let's <u>listen</u>, go, <u>hurry</u>, <u>see</u>, and <u>find</u>. Let's <u>spread</u> the Word, and let's <u>glorify</u> and <u>praise</u> God!

What does that look like in the 21st century? It means seeking Him in the Word and prayer and in relationship. Spending time develops and deepens that relationship. Then knowing Jesus better will motivate us to also introduce Him to others. And it will result in our singing His praise.

This is the Good News of Christmas! Take action! Let's hear the angel's call. Let's put on our running shoes and head to the manger.

> *He [Jesus] said to them, "Go into all the world and preach*
> *the gospel to all creation." (Mark 16:15)*

The shepherds were prompted by an angelic chorus. One of my favorite renditions of "Hark the Herald Angels Sing" is from *A Charlie Brown Christmas* when the children sing it on "loo" their heads bobbing to take a collective breath.

But the words of the song are so powerful. One of my favorite lines is "God and sinners reconciled." My kindergarten chorus and I would hold one hand high and drop the other, then bring them together in one big clap on the last syllable to demonstrate God and sinners reconciled. He was born to take on our sins so that "man no more may die" and to give us all second birth.

Hark! the herald angels sing
Glory to the newborn King
Peace on earth and mercy mild
God and sinners reconciled.
Joyful all ye nations rise
Join the triumph of the skies;
With the angelic host proclaim
Christ is born in Bethlehem'
Hark! the herald angels sing
Glory to the newborn King.

Christ by highest heaven adored
Christ the everlasting Lord
Late in time behold him come,
Offspring of a virgin's womb.
Veiled in flesh the Godhead see;
Hail, the incarnate deity,
Pleased as Man with Men to dwell,
Jesus, our Emmanuel!
Hark! the herald angels sing,
Glory to the newborn King.

Hail, the heaven-born Prince of peace!
Hail the Son of righteousness!
Light and life to all he brings,
Risen with healing in his wings.
Mild he lays his glory by,
Born that man no more may die,
Born to raise the sons of earth,
Born to give them second birth.
Hark! the herald angels sing,
Glory to the newborn King.

Prayer

Lord, the humble shepherds are a great example of listening and taking action. Help me put you first over everything else. I would like to hurry to the manger because You are there, and I want to see You! I want to know your story and tell it to many.

But Mary...

So they hurried off and found Mary and Joseph, and the baby, who was lying in the manger. When they had seen him, they spread the word concerning what had been told them about this child, and all who heard it were amazed at what the shepherds said to them. But Mary treasured up all these things and pondered them in her heart. The shepherds returned, glorifying and praising God for all the things they had heard and seen, which were just as they had been told. (Luke 2:16-20)

There's so much celebration and excitement surrounding the birth of a baby and a whole lot more questions than answers! "Did they have a girl or a boy?" "What's his name?" "How much did he weigh?" "Who does he look like?"

Once the baby is born, there is also the frenzy of friends arriving with gifts and open arms. Sometimes the mom can be overwhelmed with trying to learn how to nurse, change diapers, and swaddle her newborn. Do you suppose that could have been how young Mary felt?

The shepherds were the first visitors (but not invited by their hosts). And yet, who can question an angel's summons? The shepherds' story was so amazing to "all who heard it" (whomever that included). Yet this scriptural account is followed by a big BUT—a contrast to interrupt the hurry so we stop and take notice of Mary and the baby.

> "**But Mary** treasured up all these things and pondered them in her heart."

In other words, Mary *treasured* it: she observed the news, kept it within herself and preserved it from being lost. She *pondered* it: she brought it together so she could discuss it in her mind. She collected the pieces of the story in the very center of her being.

Tomorrow is Christmas Eve. How lovely to take time to be quiet. To think. To treasure and ponder. To collect your thoughts and reflect. To pray. To listen to music. To read God's Word. To light the Advent wreath—a circle illustrating that God has no beginning or end and His love is eternal. The greenery representing life and the candles inspire us, that just as Jesus is the light, we are to be lights to the world.

The twinkling Christmas tree also reminds us of God's love—evergreen and everlasting, the triangular shape representing the Father, Son, and Holy Spirit and pointing heavenward, the star prompting us, like the Magi, to pursue the King.[8]

What does it take to put a big BUT in your Christmas celebration? What would it take for you to STOP everything so you *can* treasure and ponder?

*Hit Pause. Take a deep breath in and exhale any tension. Pray aloud:

Prayer

Lord, help me be quiet and know that You are God. May I find my rest in You alone. May I treasure up all the things of the Christmas story and ponder them in my heart. Today I recall Psalm 62:1, "Truly my soul finds rest in God; my salvation comes from him."

All Is Calm: The Peace of God

While they were there, the time came for the baby to be born, and she gave birth to her firstborn, a son. She wrapped him in cloths and placed him in a manger, because there was no room for them in the inn (Luke 2:6–7).

And here we are at Christmas. The stable is calm, and their hopes are bright. *Calm and Bright.*

On Christmas Eve, 1818, Joseph Mohr, asked Franz Gruber to set the words of his composition "Silent Night" to music with a guitar accompaniment. According to numerous accounts, the organ at the St. Nicholas church had broken down, forcing Father Nöstler to accept a midnight mass with an alternative musical instrument. That evening Mohr and Gruber sang "Stille Nacht" accompanied by guitar with four-part chorus echoing on "Sleep in heavenly peace."

Once named "The Song from Heaven" it is perhaps most powerful when the world is not so still and silent.[9]

On December 24, 1914, the British and Germans were hunkered down in icy trenches on the Western Front. British troops saw twinkling lights near the German trenches. After looking into binoculars, they discovered the Germans were holding lighted Christmas trees above their heads. "Stille Nacht, Heilige Nacht" ("silent night, holy night") rang out, and the British joined in, singing along in English. Both sides laid aside their weapons and exchanged gifts, played soccer, and sang carols.[10]

Who wouldn't be calmed by the carol's simplicity? This ¾ time lullaby reaches for the highest note on the first "heavenly" then falls to the lowest note on the final "peace."

We all want "all is calm." We all want to know in our future "all is bright," and we want to "sleep in heavenly peace."

This is the eve of something wonderful—the eve of celebrating the nearness and closeness of Immanuel—God with us. It may not be a silent night outside or a silent night in your life, but you can find a silent night in your heart as you reflect on this "Holy infant so tender and mild."

Silent night, holy night! All is calm, all is bright.
Round yon Virgin, Mother and Child
Holy infant so tender and mild,
Sleep in heavenly peace
Sleep in heavenly peace.

Silent night, holy night! Shepherds quake at the sight.
Glories stream from heaven afar
Heavenly hosts sing Alleluia,

Christ the Savior is born!
Christ, the Savior, is born
Silent night, holy night! Son of God love's pure light
Radiant beams from Thy holy face
With the dawn of redeeming grace
Jesus Lord, at Thy birth
Jesus, Lord, at Thy birth.

Prayer

God, Your tender mercy sent Your Son—love's pure light—into the world. The infant that slept in peace is here to guide our feet into the way of peace. We sing Alleluia that He is born and has brought redeeming grace. Thank you for wrapping the newborn in love. Truly the best present ever.

Who Do You Say I Am?

No one has ever seen God, but God the One and Only, who is at the Father's side, has made him known. (John 1:18)

One of my favorite Christmas verses is John 1:18 which says that Jesus describes God. I especially like it in the Amplified version.

"No one has seen God [His essence, His divine nature] at any time; the [One and] only begotten God [that is, the unique Son] who is in the intimate presence of the Father, He has explained Him [and interpreted and revealed the awesome wonder of the Father]."

Jesus has declared, interpreted, made him known, and explained God! Now that brings us to an interesting question from author Philip Yancey in *The Jesus I Never Knew*.

If Jesus came to reveal God to us, then what do I learn about God from that first Christmas?[11]

How would you answer it?

On Christmas Day we all must ask, "Why is this particular baby so special? Why do we still celebrate His birthday? The answer to this question determines much. Indeed, *what child is this?*

William Dix, an insurance manager, is the lyricist behind a carol that raises a rhetorical question. After a life-threatening illness left him bed-ridden for months, he had the opportunity to study the Bible and write out his answer in the familiar carol, "What Child is This?" His answer? Christ the King! Son of Mary, King of Kings, Christ, Savior, and Lord.

What child is this? Jesus answered it over thirty years later. "I am the way and the truth and the life. No one comes to the Father except through me. If you really knew me, you would know my Father as well. From now on, you do know him and have seen him" (John 14:6–7). Jesus further adds, "Anyone who has seen me has seen the Father" (v. 9) and "I am in the Father and the Father is in me" (v. 11).

Jesus is clear about who He is but still asks the disciples, "Who do people say the Son of Man is?" They answered,

> *"Some say John the Baptist; others say Elijah; and still others, Jeremiah or one of the prophets." "But what about you?" he asked. "Who do you say I am?" Simon Peter answered, "You are the Messiah, the Son of the living God." (Matthew 16:13-16)*

But what about you, dear reader? What if Jesus asked you, "Who do you say I am?" Our answer to the question makes an eternal difference.

Today, take time to read Luke 2:1–20 aloud, or the entire story in chronological order beginning on page ___, or maybe let Linus read it from the movie, *A Charlie Brown Christmas* and ask others who may be listening what they learn about God from the Christmas story, then answer the question, What Child Is This?

What child is this who laid to rest on Mary's lap is sleeping?
Whom angels greet with anthems sweet while shepherds
    watch are keeping.
This, this is Christ the King whom shepherds guard and
    angels sing.
Haste, haste to bring Him laud.
The babe, the son of Mary.

Why lies He in such mean estate,
Where ox and donkeys are feeding?
Good Christians, fear, for sinners here
The silent Word is pleading.
Nails, spears shall pierce him through,
the cross he bore for me, for you.
Hail, hail the Word made flesh,
the Babe, the Son of Mary.

So bring him incense, gold, and myrrh,
Come, peasant, king, to own him.
The King of kings salvation brings,
Let loving hearts enthrone him.

Raise, raise a song on high,
The virgin sings her lullaby
Joy, joy for Christ is born,
The babe, the Son of Mary.

This, this is Christ the King,
Whom shepherds guard and angels sing:
Haste, haste to bring Him laud,
The babe, the son of Mary.

> *The Son is the radiance of God's glory and the exact repre-*
> *sentation of his being, sustaining all things by his powerful*
> *word. (Hebrews 1:3)*

Prayer

Jesus, I am thankful for Your presence in my life. That is the
greatest present of all. You came to reveal God to me. Teach
me more and more every time I open Your Word. Help me
to see You in every reading. You are the Great I Am, and I
proclaim You as Messiah, the Son of the Living God.

Waiting for the Consolation

For in this hope we were saved. But hope that is seen is no hope at all. Who hopes for what he already has? But if we hope for what we do not yet have, we wait for it patiently (Romans 8:24-25).

I used to think December 26th was the worst day of the year. But no more. Because Christmas is connected to Easter, we can celebrate Jesus—God with Us ALL YEAR. Celebrating Christ's birth is never "over."

Forty days after Jesus's birth, Joseph and Mary took the five-mile, two-hour journey to the temple in Jerusalem where they offered a burnt offering in accordance with scripture. They left two small birds, indicating their poverty. Here they would present Jesus to the Lord.

What would it mean to present God's Son to His Father? Jesus already belonged to God. He was and is God. How interesting to present Him holy before God! He was and is and will always be Holiness.

And there they met Simeon.

Simeon was given the prophecy as well as the promise that he would one day meet the Messiah.

He was waiting for the consolation of Israel, and the Holy Spirit was on him. It had been revealed to him by the Holy Spirit that he would not die before he had seen the Lord's Messiah. (Luke 2:25–26)

In *One Incredible Moment*, Max Lucado describes Simeon's looking as "waiting forwardly." Simeon was not demanding, nor hurrying; he was waiting.[12]

Someone else was at the temple. Anna had her eyes open. Anna had deep faith and hope that she would one day see the Messiah. She lived for seeing the promised Messiah, and she was not disappointed. It didn't happen in her twenties, thirties, or even her sixties or seventies. God knew the right moment and the right place.

No angel visited Anna, no star stopped over her home, and she was not invited to the manger. Instead, Jesus met Anna in the place Anna called home: the temple.

Anna experienced expectant living. We can learn from Anna and Simeon who were both "waiting forwardly." Simeon then connects the event to Easter.

Simeon prophesied to Mary and Joseph that Jesus will be a "sign that will be spoken against." Mary hears that her baby will be opposed and refused. He goes on to say, "And a sword will pierce your own soul too." She doesn't comprehend it yet, but her very breath of life will indeed be pierced when she stands beneath the cross, helplessly watching her son die. We are again reminded that Jesus's birth will always be connected to His death. But in order to be the "consolation of Israel," He will conquer death through His resurrection.

Just like Simeon, the song "The Holly and the Ivy" links Christmas with Easter. The holly's sharp points remind us of Christ's crown of thorns; the green leaves represent eternal life; the red berries point to the blood of Christ; and the bitter green bark reminds us of the cross.[13]

The holly bears a blossom, as white as lily flow'r
And Mary bore sweet Jesus Christ, to be our dear Savior.
The holly bears a berry, as red as any blood,
And Mary bore sweet Jesus Christ, to do poor sinners good.
The holy bears a prickle, as short as any thorn,
And Mary bore sweet Jesus Christ, on Christmas Day in the morn
The holly bears a bark, as bitter as the gall
And Mary bore sweet Jesus Christ, for to redeem us all.

As we move from Christmas toward a new year, and I consider New Year's resolutions, I'm reminded that almost everything on earth that I look forward to will come and go, but Jesus is eternal. Spending time with Him now, prepares me for an eternity in His presence. On your new calendar, consider writing Immanuel to remind you to celebrate Jesus through all seasons and to "wait forwardly" for His second coming.

Wait for the Lord;
be strong and take heart
and wait for the Lord. Psalm 27:14

Prayer

Jesus, I want to live waiting forwardly for You. You might come again in my lifetime, or I may first see You face to face when I leave this temporary place I call home. No matter, I will celebrate Your birth at Christmas and Your life every day, thankful that You died for me and rose again so that when my time on earth is over, I will run into your arms.

His Indescribable Gift

Every good and perfect gift is from above, coming down from the Father of the heavenly lights, who does not change like shifting shadows (James 1:17).

At Thanksgiving, the grownups in our family drew names to give one special gift to the person on their slip of paper, keeping their recipient a secret until the presents were opened. On Christmas Day, the gifts were pulled from beneath the tree, and unwrapped one by one.

My quiet Dutch grandpa sat with a present on his lap addressed To: Grandpa. At last, he opened it and announced, "Just what I always wanted!" Everyone exchanged glances as he chuckled, but no one claimed to have given this perfect gift. When he could hold it in no longer, Grandpa shyly admitted, "I drew my own name." He knew just what he wanted and gave it to himself.

When you opened your presents this Christmas, was there a gift that stood out because someone knew just what you wanted or needed? How did that person know what would please you? What did it take for him or her to give you the perfect gift? Did he or she spend time with you, observing your needs, asking questions, noting your interests? He or she must really have cared! (I'd hope that person had my name!)

Did you know God has your name? The giver of all perfect gifts knew everything about you even before you were born. He knows exactly what you need, and He desires to give it to you.

Over two thousand years ago, we received one unforgettable gift. God gave us the PERFECT gift in His Son Jesus, Immanuel, God with us. That's the best Christmas gift ever! No matter what you received this Christmas, consider accepting the eternal present, wrapped in swaddling clothes and sacrificial love. Today would also be a great day to count your blessings by listing gifts from God.

> *"Thanks be to God for his indescribable gift!" (2 Corinthians 9:15)*

Dear God—First, I want to thank you for your Son whose birthday we just celebrated. You have richly blessed my life. Today I thank you for

1.

2.

3.

4.

5.

Prayer

My dear Jesus, I thank you for the biggest decision I will ever make. I feel You calling me to be Your child. I want to follow You. Jesus. I believe You are the Son of God. Please forgive me of my sins, which sent You to the cross. Please lead me in my earthly walk. I look forward to seeing You one day in heaven.

Wise Men Came from the East

> *On coming to the house, they saw the child with his mother Mary, and they bowed down and worshiped him. Then they opened their treasures and presented him with gifts of gold and of incense and of myrrh. (Matthew 2:11)*

We three kings of Orient are
Bearing gifts we traverse afar.
Field and fountain, moor and mountain,
Following yonder star.

The first five words of "We Three Kings" hold at least three fallacies: the kings were Magi; their number unknown; and they were not from the Orient. Let's focus on some key words found in the first stanza...

THREE: Three gifts were offered, and ancient church tradition offers three names for the Magi: Caspar, Balthazar, and Melchior. In fact, there isn't any reference in the biblical account to a specific number of Magi.

KINGS: Stargazers such as the Magi blended astronomy and astrology. They looked at laws and movement but also interpretation, combining science and religion.

Medieval and Renaissance artists painted the figures in kingly robes perhaps influenced by messianic prophecy found in Psalm 72 about kings coming to bow down and give gifts of gold. Or Isaiah 60:1–6 which mentions kings, camels, gold, and incense.

ORIENT: The Magi came from the east, a journey of a thousand miles, anywhere from Arabia, Media, or most likely Persia.

The magi *did* come bearing gifts. Without a baby registry, did God tell them what to bring? The gifts could have gone unnamed, and yet Matthew lists all three.

Born a king on Bethlehem's plain,
Gold *I bring to crown Him again,*
King forever, ceasing never
Over us all to reign.

Gold was even more valuable in Jesus' time than it is now, and only given to someone of importance. Only royal children ever received gifts this extravagant. The gold may have helped fund Mary and Joseph's flight to Egypt.[14]

Frankincense to offer have I.
Incense owns a Deity nigh.
Prayer and praising all men raising,
Worship Him, God on high.

Frankincense and Myrrh, both resins extracted from trees, are collected in a process similar to how we gather maple syrup. The bark is stripped, the wood cut, then the tree's wound bleeds.

Frankincense is an antiseptic, anti-fungal, and anti-inflammatory substance and was used as a sacred incense in the temple or the Tent of Meeting. Burning incense is associated with meeting God and offering prayers to Him.[15]

Myrrh is mine: Its bitter perfume
Breaths a life of gathering gloom.
Sorrowing, sighing, bleeding dying,
Sealed in the stone-cold tomb.

Myrrh, similar in purpose to frankincense, is an aromatic, orange-colored resin, providing the scent used in anointing oils, perfumes, and embalming liquids. When Jesus died, His body was anointed with myrrh as a part of the burial process.[16] Could the Magi have comprehended the significance of their gifts honoring Jesus as king, High Priest, and victor over death?

The final verse of the carol exclaims how Christmas relates to Easter.

Glorious now behold Him arise,
King and God and Sacrifice.
Alleluia, alleluia!
Sounds through the earth and skies.

Gift giving continues to be a part of Christmas. One December, my youngest brother asked for a toy submarine, which if you inserted a pill, submerged in the bathtub. After my dad gave my other brother and me money to shop for one another, we searched the long rows at the local Pay'n'Save, hoping to find the prized deep-sea diver. Finally, we inquired of a clerk who led us down the aisle and stopped and said, "I believe it's right HERE."
It was. But sitting in the middle of the aisle, oblivious to everything but the submarine on his lap, was my little brother, the would-be-recipient.

Our dad gave him money so that he could share with others, but instead my little brother clung tightly to his own wants.

We all do that.

Our heavenly Father has richly blessed us with time and talents and money, but we sit on the floor clutching something in our lap. It might even be exactly what God wants to surprise us with at another time or place. We are called to share what God has given us in recognition of Christ.

Give, and it will be given to you. A good measure, pressed down, shaken together, and running over, will be poured into your lap. For with the measure you use, it will be measured to you. Luke 6:38

Today we learned from the Magi's generosity. These philo-sophic astrologers were wise-enough men to seek the one true King. God used them to expand the Christmas story to distant lands and to remind us that not only was the good news of the Messiah given to poor, lowly shepherds, but to these wealthy and learned non-Jews.

The Magi gave of their time, money, and energy to find the King and to bow down and worship Him. What about us, today?

Prayer

Lord, show me where and how to share the gifts you've given me. Let me not focus on my own desires, but may I look to the needs of others. Help me have an open hand and an open heart so that I am generous and giving to all.

A Star Will Come

> A star will come out of Jacob;
>   a scepter will rise out of Israel. (Numbers 24:17)

Our local preschool Christmas program listed one little boy in a unique debut role. I could hardly wait to tell his mom, "Colin is the STAR of the show!" Indeed, her son was playing the star over the Nativity.

Many have tried to explain the phenomenon of the star. Was it a comet, the planet Venus, a supernova, a conjunction of planets, a pause in planetary orbit, or perhaps even Halley's Comet, which actually appeared in approximately 12 BC. A star hovering over the birthplace of the Son of God was definitely supernatural.[17]

But then again, given all the other amazing miracles in the Christmas story, why does a supernatural occurrence created by God seem so contrived? After all, "He determines the number of the stars and calls them each by name" (Psalm 147:4).

Couldn't the God who created and placed the stars in the sky, and who knows them by name, also create a star of wonder to lead a group of mathematicians away from their past and toward a glorious new hope in Christ? God led the Israelites with a pillar of fire by night and a cloud by day toward their Promised Land! What would be so difficult about creating a single star to guide seekers to the Perfect Light?

When we approach a new year, we look for guidance. It might be nice to have a star to lead us everywhere we go. A guide to make sure we are directed to Jesus and spend our days well. "Teach us to number our days aright, that we may gain a heart of wisdom" (Psalm 90:12).

We have exactly that guidance in the Holy Spirit:

> And I will ask the Father, and he will give you another advocate to help you and be with you forever—the Spirit of truth. The world cannot accept him, because it neither sees him nor knows him. But you know him, for he lives with you and will be in you. (John 14:16–17)

> But the Advocate, the Holy Spirit, whom the Father will send in my name, will teach you all things and will remind you of everything I have said to you. (John 14:26)

> But when he, the Spirit of truth, comes, he will guide you into all the truth. He will not speak on his own; he will speak only what he hears, and he will tell you what is yet to come. (John 16:13)

Not only do we have the Holy Spirit who understands our needs even when all we can do is groan, we have the Word, a book full of wisdom to guide us.

There are so many online Bible reading plans that can be a lamp for our feet and a light unto our path. For the new year, you might want to check out navigators.org, oneyearbibleonline, YouVersion, Bible Project Online, First5.org, There are plenty of Bible apps that can help you wake up with Good News!

Yesterday we looked at the verses of "We Three Kings," but not the chorus, which is about the "star of the show."

Star of Wonder, Star of Light.
Star with royal beauty bright.
Westward leading, still proceeding,
Guide us to Thy perfect light.

God's Word has many verses about the stars. Read them aloud tonight when the sky fills with stars and then sing the chorus of "We Three Kings."

Lift up your eyes and look to the heavens:
  Who created all these?
He who brings out the starry host one by one
  and calls forth each of them by name.
Because of his great power and mighty strength,
  not one of them is missing. (Isaiah 40:26)

By the word of the Lord the heavens were made,
their starry host by the breath of his mouth. (Psalm 33:6)

The heavens declare the glory of God;
the skies proclaim the work of his hands. (Psalm 19:1)

When I consider your heavens,
the work of your fingers,
the moon and the stars,
which you have set in place,
what is mankind that you are mindful of them,
human beings that you care for them? (Psalm 8:3-4)

"I, Jesus, have sent my angel to give you this testimony for
the churches.
I am the Root and the Offspring of David,
and the bright Morning Star." (Revelation 22:16)

Prayer

Lord, I marvel at the works of Your hands, and what you have set in place. The heavens do declare Your glory, and the skies proclaim the works of Your hands. Who am I that you are mindful of me and care for me? And yet you do. You want me to follow You. Your word will light my feet and my path. May I seek it for direction and may I gain a heart of wisdom. Lead me through this next year and help me faithfully follow you every day.

Herod Became Furious

When they had gone, an angel of the Lord appeared to Joseph in a dream. "Get up," he said, "take the child and his mother and escape to Egypt. Stay there until I tell you, for Herod is going to search for the child to kill him."

So he got up, took the child and his mother during the night and left for Egypt, where he stayed until the death of Herod. And so was fulfilled what the Lord had said through the prophet: "Out of Egypt I called my son."

When Herod realized that he had been outwitted by the Magi, he was furious, and he gave orders to kill all the boys in Bethlehem and its vicinity who were two years old and under, in accordance with the time he had learned from the Magi. Then what was said through the prophet Jeremiah was fulfilled:

> *"A voice is heard in Ramah,*
> *weeping and great mourning,*
> *Rachel weeping for her children*
> *and refusing to be comforted,*
> *because they are no more." (Matthew 2:13–18)*

Every story needs an antagonist, and Herod takes on that role. At Christmas, it's not pleasant to read about violence.

But knowing what happened helps us understand the angel's warnings to Joseph, Mary and Joseph's subsequent flights, and how God protected the little family.

Herod was the ruler of Judea and was also known for the impressive architecture constructed with Jewish labor. His own multi-storied, fortress-like palace called the Herodium sat on a hill overlooking the region.[18]

But Herod's personal life was a mess. He married ten times, and called for the execution of one wife, as well as his uncle, mother-in-law, father-in-law, his three sons, Antipater, Aristobulus and Alexander, his barber, and a close friend. He also had the high priest and his brother-in-law drowned.[19] Five days before Herod died, he arrested three thousand of Jerusalem's respected citizens, commanding their execution upon his death to ensure mourning on that day—even if it wasn't for him.[20]

Herod's referral to Jesus as King of the Jews and Christ ("Anointed One," "Messiah"), is intriguing. Herod and the Magi acknowledge the title of Jesus, but while Herod the "not-so-great" felt jealous and threatened by the King of the Jews, the Magi worshiped the child and bowed down before Him.

To wipe out any possibility a new baby could challenge his power, Herod destroyed all children in the region two years of age and under—including his own son. Though death toll estimates range from two hundred to two thousand, it is more realistic to estimate thirty to sixty children in a village of three hundred. Losing one tenth of Bethlehem's population would have meant extreme grief and mourning, [21]and is worthy of this mournful carol.

Set in a minor key, this haunting "Lully, Lullay, Thou Little Tiny Child" lullaby is also called "Coventry Carol" because the local Coventry, England crafts guild performed a pageant depicting Herod's slaughter. Mothers in the performance sing the children to sleep so Herod's soldiers can't find them.

Lully, thou little, tiny child
Bye bye, lully, lullay
Lully, Thou little tiny Child
Bye bye, lully, lullay

O sisters too, how may we do for to preserve this day
This poor youngling for whom we sing
Bye bye, lully, lullay?

Herod the king, in his raging, charged he hath this day
His men of might in his own sight all children young to slay.

Then woe is me, poor child, for thee and ever mourn and say
For thy parting nor say nor sing,
Bye bye, lully, lullay.

As Jesus Christ later hung on the cross, the written charge was posted in Greek, Hebrew, Aramaic, and Latin identifying Him as **King of the Jews.** Those around him mocked him **as King of Israel** and **Messiah**. They had the right name, but they didn't know Him. They missed out on a relationship with the one who begged His Father to forgive them, and who taught us all to love our enemies and pray for those who persecute.

I hope and pray that you know the Jesus who was not just born, but who lived, died, and rose again. That He is your King and Savior and friend. That you respond like the Magi and not King Herod. How sad it would be to celebrate Christmas without truly knowing the one having the birthday. The one who came to bring love. But what joy there is when we do follow Him.

Prayer

Jesus, I know who You are. I know that You died for me and because You rose again, I can have eternal life with You. There is so much hurt and evil in the world and people that are hurting or doing things that hurt others. I pray, Lord for all of them. That they could come to imitate You, follow Your example of love, and truly recognize that You are the Christ, the King of Israel, the Anointed One, and the Messiah.

Let Us Kneel

> Come, let us bow down in worship, let us kneel before the
> Lord our maker, for he is our God and we are the people of
> his pasture, the flock under his care (Psalm 95:6-7a).

In the village of Greccio, Italy in 1223, St. Francis of Assisi arranged the first nativity scene. At an outdoor candlelight mass, the monks from the religious order sang, and the townspeople gathered near the manger with candles and torches for a new and inspiring worship experience. Each year this scene is recreated in that same Italian village.[22]

Nativity displays continue to fascinate young and old. Every family should have a simple set so little children can move the figures to the manger.

In *The Nativity Alive*, carolers vandalize an outdoor nativity set, and one little caroler lingers to meet Mr. Crouch, the elderly owner of the display. As Mr. Crouch illuminates each nativity figurine, the statues come to life and relate their own stories in drama and song. When our church produced the pageant, it was my hope that the musical would cause children and adults to contemplate the perspective of each nativity character.

Today as the year ends and the Christmas narrative concludes, let's do just that and review each character.

Herod asked where the Christ was to be found. He knew about a king, and yet unlike the Magi who traveled great distances, he wouldn't go five miles to find Him. He believed enough to fear, but he didn't believe enough to go and see. To follow. Neither did anyone else in Jerusalem.[23] They could have met *God with us*. Instead, they stayed away or tried to kill Him. They lost a relationship that would have lasted for eternity.

Do we watch others travel toward Christ while we stay behind?

Or are we like the shepherds? We've heard exciting news, and our new faith is so on fire, we run and share the Good News.

Or perhaps our journey of faith is more like Joseph's: one of trust and obedience, day by day leaving what is comfortable to do whatever the Lord commands?

Or maybe like Mary's, whose faith was immediate and humble? Or are we more like Elizabeth, who retreated to contemplate the miracle within? Though she had never entered the Holy of Holies and never spoken with an angel, she had a mature faith that recognized and believed what was happening around her.

Or maybe we're like Zechariah, who is speechless because he couldn't quite get his mind around the most amazing encounter of his life?

Maybe we're more like Simeon and Anna and show faith by waiting and believing without having seen. We know God is working in our lives and that Jesus is our hope.

Then there's the Magi. We've heard all about the Christ child, and we are moving on a journey closer to our Savior. When we meet Him, we believe, and accept Him as Lord. We bow down before Him in worship and praise the name above all names.

Do you relate to any of these characters? If you have a nativity set or a picture of the nativity, can you imagine yourself at the manger? Move closer today and every day to the baby who would be King.

There is room at the manger for you. Is there room in your heart for Jesus?

This less familiar carol "Thou Didst Leave Thy Royal Throne" recognizes Christ's kingship. The lyrics include his life and His death, ending with a powerful declaration that I hope we can all proclaim! "O come to my heart, Lord Jesus, There is room in my heart for Thee."

Thou didst leave Thy throne and Thy kingly crown,
When Thou camest to earth for me;
But in Bethlehem's home was there found no room
For Thy holy nativity.
O come to my heart, Lord Jesus,
There is room in my heart for Thee.
Heaven's arches rang when the angels sang,
Proclaiming Thy royal degree;
But of lowly birth didst Thou come to earth,
And in great humility.
O come to my heart, Lord Jesus,
There is room in my heart for Thee.
The foxes found rest, and the birds their nest
In the shade of the forest tree;
But Thy couch was the sod, O Thou Son of God,
In the deserts of Galilee.
O come to my heart, Lord Jesus,
There is room in my heart for Thee.
Thou camest, O Lord, with the living word
That should set Thy people free;
But with mocking scorn, and with crown of thorn,
They bore Thee to Calvary.
O come to my heart, Lord Jesus,
There is room in my heart for Thee.
When the heavens shall ring, and the angels sing,
At Thy coming to victory
Let Thy voice call me home, saying "Yet there is room,

There is room at My side for thee."
My heart shall rejoice, Lord Jesus,
When Thou comest and callest for me.

Prayer

*Dear Lord, I can learn from all the characters in the Christmas
story. Help my faith to grow into a deep and abiding walk
with You. O come to my heart, Lord Jesus,
There is room in my heart for Thee.*

God's Will

> *In the beginning was the Word, and the Word was with God,*
> *and the Word was God. He was with God in the beginning.*
> *Through him all things were made; without him nothing was*
> *made that has been made. In him was life, and that life was*
> *the light of all mankind. The light shines in the darkness,*
> *and the darkness has not overcome it. (John 1:1-4)*

My husband Will and I flew from Seattle to return home to Virginia, arriving on New Year's Eve, just in time to pray in the New Year with friends. When we walked into their home, someone called out, "We were just praying for God's will, and look who came in the door!" There were more than two or three gathered in prayer and now much laughter. For indeed, on a blind date a decade earlier, I'd found "God's Will" for my life.

In all seriousness, "God's will" is something we all desire but seem to feel the need to focus on especially as we enter a new year. For some sort of goal or sail and keel for our ship, we make resolutions to keep us heading in the right direction.

Sometimes we hope for a voice from heaven. We long for confirmations, perhaps not unlike Mary and Joseph received. An angel spoke to both individually. When Mary arrived at Elizabeth's, she was greeted as the mother of Jesus. Such confirmation! The shepherds came running to Bethlehem in search of what the angel foretold. Joseph and Mary must have been in awe. Simeon and Anna recognized Jesus as the Son of God. The Magi followed a unique star and arrived bearing gifts for a King. That's a lot of confirmation.

There are so many books on discerning the will of God, but the best book is right in front of us. We have the Word made flesh who spoke what we need in Scriptures. We just need to *apply* daily what we *read* daily. Rinse and repeat.

> *The Word became flesh and made his dwelling among us. We have seen his glory, the glory of the one and only Son, who came from the Father, full of grace and truth. (John 1:14)*

> *In the past God spoke to our ancestors through the prophets at many times and in various ways, but in these last days he has spoken to us by his Son, whom he appointed heir of all things, and through whom also he made the universe. (Hebrews 1:1-2)*

Where should we start? Beginning with God's Son Jesus's own instruction and important commandments are a great place: To love the Lord and love our neighbor.

Jesus encourages us to follow His example of love, and it will bring us joy.

> *If you keep my commands, you will remain in my love, just as I have kept my Father's commands and remain in his love. I have told you this so that my joy may be in you and that your joy may be complete. My command is this: Love each other as I have loved you. (John 15:10–12)*

Need to talk to someone? We have the privilege of coming directly to the Lord in prayer.

> *Let us then approach God's throne of grace with confidence, so that we may receive mercy and find grace to help us in our time of need. (Hebrews 4:16)*

> *We have an advocate with the Father—Jesus Christ, the Righteous One. (1 John 2:1).*

> *When and how often should we pray?*

> *Rejoice always, pray continually, give thanks in all circumstances; for this is **God's will** for you in Christ Jesus. (1 Thessalonians 5:16–18, emphasis added).*

We also have the privilege of fellowshipping with Christian brothers and sisters who can offer wisdom and encouragement.

> *And let us consider how we may spur one another on toward love and good deeds, not giving up meeting together, as some are in the habit of doing, but encouraging one another—and all the more as you see the Day approaching (Hebrews 10:24-25).*

Also,

> *Let the message of Christ dwell among you richly as you teach and admonish one another with all wisdom through psalms, hymns, and songs from the Spirit, singing to God with gratitude in your hearts. (Colossians 3:16)*

All of these are compasses to guide your decisions and choices into the next year so you will walk with Him in love and truth.

- Read God's Word
- Imitate Jesus and know His teachings
- Pray
- Gather with Christians to worship

Prayer

Lord, I'm not always sure what to do next. But sometimes I look for Your will when it's right in front of me in Your Word and in the example of the Word made flesh. Help me follow the Word you've given me as I seek to follow You all the days of my life. May I not give up gathering with other believers but come together and encourage and find encouragement with other Christians, that we may spur one another to loving actions that glorify You. This will give our lives on earth purpose and a plan to please You.

New Every Morning

Therefore, if anyone is in Christ, he is a new creation; the old has gone, the new has come! (2 Corinthians 5:17)

On December 3, 1929, my grandparents fled Stalin's Russia. My grandma's second-born son had just died; her husband Nikolai had been arrested for his religious beliefs. All her clothing had been taken; her three-year-old firstborn son, Kolya, had been deported hundreds of miles away, and Lena had just given birth to her baby Abe in a Moscow hospital. To stay alive, they had to flee, leaving Kolya behind.

My grandparents spent that Christmas in a German refugee camp, relieved, but grieving. There had been over 17,000 Germans. Out of the 5,761 refugees that escaped Moscow in 1929, only four were allowed into the U.S.

Two years after their escape, their five-year-old son Kolya traveled solo most of the way from the Crimean Peninsula to America to be reunited with his family in McCook, Nebraska.

In a life filled with miraculous God-incidents, my grandparents claimed their life verse: "Because of the Lord's great love we are not consumed, for his compassions never fail.

They are new every morning; great is your faithfulness"
(Lamentations 3:22–23).

What verse shall we claim? With the flip of a page, we came to the end of one calendar and need a new one. How shall we fill in the blanks?

A college friend posted a sign above his door. It read:

FOR ME TO LIVE IS_____.

Every day when he left his room, he had to fill in the blank from Philippians 1:21: "For to me, to live is Christ."

Consider finding a verse for this year. Here are a few to consider:

> *Trust in the LORD with all your heart*
>   *and lean not on your own understanding;*
> *in all your ways submit to him,*
>   *and he will make your paths straight (Proverbs 3:5–6)*

> *But they that wait upon the LORD shall renew their strength;*
> *they shall mount up with wings as eagles; they shall run,*
> *and not be weary; and they shall walk, and not faint. (Isaiah 40:11)*

> *Finally, brothers and sisters, whatever is true, whatever is noble, whatever is right, whatever is pure, whatever is lovely,*

*whatever is admirable—if anything is excellent or praisewor-
thy—think about such things. (Philippians 4:8)*

*So then, just as you received Christ Jesus as Lord, continue
to live your lives in him, rooted and built up in him, strength-
ened in the faith as you were taught, and overflowing with
thankfulness. (Colossians 2:6–7)*

*Since, then, you have been raised with Christ, set your
hearts on things above, where Christ is, seated at the right
hand of God. Set your minds on things above, not on earthly
things. (Colossians 3:1–2)*

*Therefore, as God's chosen people, holy and dearly loved,
clothe yourselves with compassion, kindness, humility,
gentleness and patience. Bear with each other and forgive
one another if any of you has a grievance against someone.
Forgive as the Lord forgave you. And over all these virtues
put on love, which binds them all together in perfect unity.
Let the peace of Christ rule in your hearts, since as members of one body you were called to peace. And be thankful.
(Colossians 3:12–15)*

*May the God of hope fill you with all joy and peace as you
trust in him, so that you may overflow with hope by the
power of the Holy Spirit. (Romans 15:13)*

Print the verse (s) you select on a notecard. Tape the
notecard to your mirror. Carry one in your purse or

briefcase. Hold it in your heart and let the Word change you from the inside out.

Proverbs 7:1–3

My son, keep my words
and store up my commands within you.
Keep my commands and you will live;
guard my teachings as the apple of your eye.
Bind them on your fingers;
write them on the tablet of your heart.

Prayer

Lord, as I look at the old calendar, thank you for everything you have done in my past and present and what you will do in my future. I will keep Your words, store Your commands, and guard Your teaching. May I write Your Words on my heart so I live them out each day of this new calendar year.

Call Forth Songs of Joy!

Let the rivers clap their hands, let the mountains sing together for joy; let them sing before the Lord, for he comes to judge the earth. He will judge the world in righteousness and the peoples with equity. (Psalm 98:8–9)

The carol "Joy to the World!" paraphrases the above scripture, calling for all of creation to joyfully praise the reign of the Lord.

Isaac Watts, the man who brought us this joy-filled song, was frustrated by the dreary archaic hymns of his day. His father challenged him to come up with a hymn that expressed joy. He succeeded by writing a new hymn for 266 Sundays, totaling 600 hymns in his lifetime!

"Joy to the World" is delightfully "singable" because it moves stepwise. Any child with little fingers on a piano can start on a high "C" and play a downward scale for the opening of the carol. Many of the succeeding phrases also have upward and downward stepwise motion.

But ironically, there is little in this carol about Christmas. The original title was actually "The Messiah's Coming and Kingdom." (Doesn't have the same ring, does it?) Though the first verse is often used in the context of Jesus's first coming, most of the carol declares Jesus's second coming. And "Let every heart prepare Him room," still happens every day! We can make room for Jesus and to sing His praise.

Joy to the world, the Lord is come!
Let earth receive her King;
Let every heart prepare Him room,
And heaven and nature sing.
Joy to the world, the Savior reigns!
Let men their songs employ;
While fields and floods, rocks, hills and plains,
Repeat the sounding joy
No more let sins and sorrows grow,
Nor thorns infest the ground;
He comes to make His blessings flow,
Far as the curse is found,
He rules the world with truth and grace,
And makes the nations prove
The glories of His righteousness,
And wonders of His love

His kingship means He will reign in glory, truth, and righteousness. Satan will be bound, and Christ's kingdom will have no end! This is a song to celebrate all year long as we anticipate His second coming.

> *The whole earth is filled with awe at your wonders; where morning dawns, where evening fades, you call forth songs of joy." Psalm 65:8*

Prayer

Jesus, You rule the world and prove your righteousness and love. Today and every day I want to receive You and prepare room for you in my heart and life. I want to sing Your praise for You reign in my heart as Savior and Lord.

Blessed Are the Peacemakers

Peacemakers who sow in peace reap a harvest of righteousness. (James 3:18)

**I don't want to end
the year on bad terms with
anyone.**

Apologize to me.

It's tough to be the first to say, "I'm sorry." When my husband and I were first married and argued, I would suddenly blurt out, "I forgive you!" After we had kids, I never enjoyed playing referee to my dueling daughters when one claimed, "But she did it to me first!" It was always a relief when they apologized, forgave one another, and started fresh.

But forgiveness and reconciliation are not as simple as they appear in ninety-minute Christmas specials where estranged family members allow walls of anger and bitterness to crumble, reconnecting just in time for a peace-filled Christmas.

Experiencing peace is a blessing. We can be peacemakers by asking forgiveness, by accepting forgiveness, and by forgiving others. That involves putting aside our differences, letting go, and letting God.

> *This is what the Sovereign Lord, the Holy One of Israel, says:*
>
> *"In repentance and rest is your salvation,*
>   *in quietness and trust is your strength, (Isaiah 30:15a)*

In this new year, keep your accounts short. "If it is possible, as far as it depends on you, live at peace with everyone" (Romans 12:18). May your answers be gentle so that they turn away anger (Proverbs 15:1), and if you feel angry, don't go to bed without resolution (Ephesians 4:26).

Give yourself the gift of forgiveness, and you will be a healthier person emotionally, spiritually, and possibly even physically.

Is there someone in your life with whom you are estranged? Let this be the year of healing. Step out in humility and say, "I'm sorry," when you think, "But she did it to me, first!" Ask forgiveness and start fresh.

Forgive immediately so you can get on with your life. I love Marianne Williamson's quote: "Unforgiveness is like drinking poison yourself and waiting for the other person to die." The saddest people I know are those poisoned by hatred and the inability to forgive. If you're holding out, unwilling to forgive, do it immediately so your Father in heaven will also forgive you (Matthew 6:15).

God called us to be peacemakers, a promised blessing from the Wonderful Counselor, Almighty God, Everlasting Father, Prince of Peace.

Blessed are the peacemakers, for they will be called sons of God. (Matthew 5:9)

Prayer

Jesus, help me forgive quickly. On the cross you forgave those who hurt you. Help me ask forgiveness and also accept the forgiveness of others. You forgave all my sins and reconciled me to God. Thank you, Jesus, for that freeing gift. May I live and forgive like You.

Build Each Other Up

Do not let any unwholesome talk come out of your mouths, but only what is helpful for building others up according to their needs, that it may benefit those who listen (Ephesians 4:29)

One wintry night in western Washington we were surprised with a snowy wonderland. My twenty-something brothers, their friends, and I celebrated by building the biggest snowmen ever.

We were kids again rolling enormous balls of snow, hefting, then stacking them taller than our height. Our creations were full of personality, wearing jewelry, scarves, and hats. We dubbed them Winston and Maggie. Winston with his moustache, and Maggie with her earrings and apron, posed proudly, delighting passersby, who slowed to see the statues— many returning with cameras.

That evening as we played Monopoly by the fire, we heard suspicious noises outside. Much to our dismay, vandals had run through the front yard, toppling our sculptures. Couldn't they appreciate the beauty of our creation? Our holiday spirit disappeared as we piled in a friend's truck to track them down. Thankfully, we never found the culprits, sparing them a tongue lashing for their cruelty and destruction.

That night, as I slept, I was awakened by voices in the front yard. "They were so neat. I can't believe someone would do that. Let's try to build them back up!" And for the next few minutes, new visitors attempted to restack, reshape, and rebuild our creations.

In the warmth of my childhood bedroom, and in the depth of my heart, a piece of Christmas—and yes, the "peace" of Christmas returned. Although one peek on Christmas morning told me Winston and Maggie could never be fully restored, I was encouraged that others appreciated and cared enough about our creations to rebuild them.

I learned a very important lesson that day: It is much easier to tear down than to build up. And once something is torn down, the damage is not always repairable.

How can we build others up? There are so many ways to encourage others: write #3 somewhere to remind yourself to compliment three people every day; contact a former teacher and express your appreciation; call someone who lives alone; plan to be a secret angel in January; bring together old friends on a Zoom call; leave a note and a little gift for a neighbor or bring Valentine cookies for someone who needs love.

> *Therefore encourage one another and build each other up.*
> *(1 Thessalonians 5:11a)*

Prayer

Lord, help me encourage and build up someone today. Someone may be holding onto a hidden hurt in quiet anguish. Whom will I meet today that needs a special word? May the words of my mouth be pleasing to You and inspire someone to want to know You more for You love Your creation.

Carry It On to Completion

*Being confident of this, that he who began a good work
in you will carry it on to completion until the day of Christ
Jesus (Philippians 1:6).*

The twelve days of Christmas actually begin on Christmas
Day and end on January 6 with Epiphany. Twelve days
to elongate the season sounds great to me! Epiphany,
which means "manifestation" or "glorious appearance,"
acknowledges the arrival and manifestations of Jesus and
formerly was the occasion Christ's birth was celebrated.
Epiphany acknowledges the arrival of the Magi or "Three
Kings' Day."

One January, I had an epiphany (a different definition!) My
toddlers taught me that Christmas goes on and on and on.
As three-year-old Christine rode through the grocery store
in my shopping cart, she suddenly belted out, BE NEAR ME
LORD JESUS, I ASK THEE TO PRAY!"

"Away in a Manger" couldn't have sounded sweeter.

Christine not only loved the music, but she also loved the
decorated Christmas tree. She turned the sometimes-
depressing task of taking down the tree into a delight and
enjoyed the privilege of "legally" removing the ornaments,

cherishing each one and the story it told. "Ooooooooo this one is sooooooo cute it makes me want to cry!" And when she accidentally broke one, she did cry.

After the tree was bare, it stood for a day or two in our living room. One-year-old Julia was distressed by the missing angel, and Christine said, "I like it better with the lights and ornaments." When the tree was dragged to the far lower pasture, Christine kept talking about the tree, and I feared she would never get over the loss.

"There's the Christmas tree!" she called out one morning.

Oh dear, I thought, now she's imagining things. However, during a ferocious windstorm, the tree had blown up and onto our front walk. As we investigated the new arrival, Christine whispered, "It's sleeping."

She continued to play with her "untibbity" (nativity) set, making characters talk, carrying the angel everywhere she went, and fighting with her little sister over Baby Jesus.

Finally, one day Christine asked almost hopefully, "Is Jesus on the cross now?" Her question helped me realize how much we want to continue celebrating His life, and that finding Jesus in everything must linger beyond Christmas.

To extend the holidays, enjoy your favorite carols once more while you pack the boxes of ornaments. You could also begin a January 6 Epiphany tradition of searching for one last present hidden in the tree. (Added incentive for family members to help with the undecorating!) Once the tree is outside, you could redecorate your tree with edible ornaments (literally for the birds)! Finish off your leftover candy cane crushed over a brownie and whipped cream!

Now might be a good time to explain how the candy cane is the shape of a shepherd's crook. The white color represents Christ's purity, and the red symbolize the stripes He received when whipped by Roman soldiers, tying Christmas to Easter. If you flip the candy cane upside down, it forms the letter "J" for Jesus.[24]

Store the Christmas cards in a basket and pull one out each day to pray for the sender, then recycle the cards by creating gift tags and post cards for next Christmas.

Valentine's Day, with fourteen days leading up to it, is coming and you can feature a countdown or links of love with the LOVE verses from 1 Corinthians 13, focusing on one aspect per day.

Love is patient
Love is kind
Love does not envy
Love does not boast, it is not proud
Love does not dishonor others
Love is not self-seeking

Love is not easily angered
Love keeps no record of wrongs
Love does not delight in evil but rejoices with the truth
Love always protects
Love always trusts
Love always hopes
Love always perseveres
Love never fails

The Lenten Season begins shortly after Valentine's Day. That's another direct connection to Christmas. With Valentine's, Easter, and even Thanksgiving, continue to celebrate and adore Him all year long. O come let us all adore Him!

O Come let us adore him,
O come let us adore him
O come let us adore Him, Christ the lord.

Prayer

Jesus, thank you for coming for me. For arriving in such a humble manner, living a simple life, and dying for me. Thank You for conquering death to rise again so that one day I might, too. May the celebrations of Christmas continue throughout the year for You and Your love are eternal.

THE CHRISTMAS STORY from Matthew, Mark, Luke, and John combined in CHRONOLOGICAL ORDER (minus genealogies which can be found in Matthew 1:1–17, and Luke 3:23–38).

The Word Became Flesh

Mark 1:11

THE BEGINNING of the GOOD NEWS about JESUS the Messiah, the Son of God!

John 1:1-3

[1] In the beginning was the Word, and the Word was with God, and the Word was God. [2] He was with God in the beginning. [3] Through him all things were made; without him nothing was made that has been made.

Luke 1:1-79

[1] Many have undertaken to draw up an account of the things that have been fulfilled among us, [2] just as they were handed down to us by those who from the first were eyewitnesses and servants of the word. [3] With this in mind, since I myself have carefully investigated everything from the beginning, I too decided to write an orderly account for you, most excellent Theophilus, [4] so that you may know the certainty of the things you have been taught.

Zechariah and Elizabeth

[5] *In the time of Herod king of Judea there was a priest named Zechariah, who belonged to the priestly division of Abijah; his wife Elizabeth was also a descendant of Aaron.* [6] *Both of them were righteous in the sight of God, observing all the Lord's commands and decrees blamelessly.* [7] *But they were childless because Elizabeth was not able to conceive, and they were both very old.*

[8] *Once when Zechariah's division was on duty and he was serving as priest before God,* [9] *he was chosen by lot, according to the custom of the priesthood, to go into the temple of the Lord and burn incense.* [10] *And when the time for the burning of incense came, all the assembled worshipers were praying outside.*

[11] *Then an angel of the Lord appeared to him, standing at the right side of the altar of incense.* [12] *When Zechariah saw him, he was startled and was gripped with fear.* [13] *But the angel said to him: "Do not be afraid, Zechariah; your prayer has been heard. Your wife Elizabeth will bear you a son, and you are to call him John.* [14] *He will be a joy and delight to you, and many will rejoice because of his birth,* [15] *for he will be great in the sight of the Lord. He is never to take wine or other fermented drink, and he will be filled with the Holy Spirit even before he is born.* [16] *He will bring back many of the people of Israel to the Lord their God.* [17] *And he will go*

on before the Lord, in the spirit and power of Elijah, to turn the hearts of the parents to their children and the disobedient to the wisdom of the righteous—to make ready a people prepared for the Lord."

Zechariah asked the angel, "How can I be sure of this? I am an old man and my wife is well along in years."

The angel said to him, "I am Gabriel. I stand in the presence of God, and I have been sent to speak to you and to tell you this good news. 20 *And now you will be silent and not able to speak until the day this happens, because you did not believe my words, which will come true at their appointed time."*

21 *Meanwhile, the people were waiting for Zechariah and wondering why he stayed so long in the temple.* 22 *When he came out, he could not speak to them. They realized he had seen a vision in the temple, for he kept making signs to them but remained unable to speak.*

23 *When his time of service was completed, he returned home.* 24 *After this his wife Elizabeth became pregnant and for five months remained in seclusion.* 25 *"The Lord has done this for me," she said. "In these days he has shown his favor and taken away my disgrace among the people."*

The Angel Gabriel Visits Mary

[26] *In the sixth month of Elizabeth's pregnancy, God sent the angel Gabriel to Nazareth, a town in Galilee,* [27] *to a virgin pledged to be married to a man named Joseph, a descendant of David. The virgin's name was Mary.* [28] *The angel went to her and said, "Greetings, you who are highly favored! The Lord is with you."*

[29] *Mary was greatly troubled at his words and wondered what kind of greeting this might be.* [30] *But the angel said to her, "Do not be afraid, Mary; you have found favor with God.* [31] *You will conceive and give birth to a son, and you are to call him Jesus.* [32] *He will be great and will be called the Son of the Most High. The Lord God will give him the throne of his father David,* [33] *and he will reign over Jacob's descendants forever; his kingdom will never end."*

"How will this be," Mary asked the angel, "since I am a virgin?"

The angel answered, "The Holy Spirit will come on you, and the power of the Most High will overshadow you. So the holy one to be born will be called the Son of God. [36] *Even Elizabeth your relative is going to have a child in her old age, and she who was said to be unable to conceive is in her sixth month.* [37] *For no word from God will ever fail."*

"I am the Lord's servant," Mary answered. "May your word to me be fulfilled." Then the angel left her.

Mary Visits Elizabeth

At that time Mary got ready and hurried to a town in the hill country of Judea, ⁴⁰ *where she entered Zechariah's home and greeted Elizabeth.* ⁴¹ *When Elizabeth heard Mary's greeting, the baby leaped in her womb, and Elizabeth was filled with the Holy Spirit.* ⁴² *In a loud voice she exclaimed: "Blessed are you among women, and blessed is the child you will bear!* ⁴³ *But why am I so favored, that the mother of my Lord should come to me?* ⁴⁴ *As soon as the sound of your greeting reached my ears, the baby in my womb leaped for joy.* ⁴⁵ *Blessed is she who has believed that the Lord would fulfill his promises to her!"*

Mary's Song

And Mary said:

⁴⁷ *"My soul glorifies the Lord*
and my spirit rejoices in God my Savior, ⁴⁸
for he has been mindful
of the humble state of his servant.

From now on all generations will call me blessed,
for the Mighty One has done great things for me—
holy is his name.

His mercy extends to those who fear him, from generation to generation.

He has performed mighty deeds with his arm;
he has scattered those who are proud in their inmost thoughts.

He has brought down rulers from their thrones but has lifted up the humble.

He has filled the hungry with good things but has sent the rich away empty.

He has helped his servant Israel,
remembering to be merciful
to Abraham and his descendants forever,
just as he promised our ancestors."

Mary stayed with Elizabeth for about three months and then returned home.

Elizabeth Gives Birth to John

When it was time for Elizabeth to have her baby, she gave birth to a son. [58] *Her neighbors and relatives heard that the Lord had shown her great mercy, and they shared her joy.*

[59] *On the eighth day they came to circumcise the child, and they were going to name him after his father Zechariah,* [60] *but his mother spoke up and said, "No! He is to be called John."*

They said to her, "There is no one among your relatives who has that name."

[62] Then they made signs to his father, to find out what he would like to name the child. [63] He asked for a writing tablet, and to everyone's astonishment he wrote, "His name is John." [64] Immediately his mouth was opened and his tongue set free, and he began to speak, praising God. [65] All the neighbors were filled with awe, and throughout the hill country of Judea people were talking about all these things. [66] Everyone who heard this wondered about it, asking, "What then is this child going to be?" For the Lord's hand was with him.

Zechariah's Song

His father Zechariah was filled with the Holy Spirit and prophesied:

*"Praise be to the Lord, the God of Israel,
because he has come to his people and redeemed them.*

He has raised up a horn of salvation for us in the house of his servant David

*[70] (as he said through his holy prophets of long ago),
[71] salvation from our enemies
and from the hand of all who hate us—
[72] to show mercy to our ancestors*

and to remember his holy covenant,
    [73] the oath he swore to our father Abraham:
[74] to rescue us from the hand of our enemies,
    and to enable us to serve him without fear
      [75] in holiness and righteousness before him all our days.

[76] And you, my child, will be called a prophet of the Most High;
    for you will go on before the Lord to prepare the way for him,
[77] to give his people the knowledge of salvation
    through the forgiveness of their sins,
[78] because of the tender mercy of our God,
    by which the rising sun will come to us from heaven
[79] to shine on those living in darkness
    and in the shadow of death,
    to guide our feet into the path of peace."

The Story of Joseph and Mary

Matthew 1:18-25

[18] This is how the birth of Jesus the Messiah came about: His mother Mary was pledged to be married to Joseph, but before they came together, she was found to be pregnant through the Holy Spirit. [19] Because Joseph her husband was faithful to the law, and yet did not want to expose her to public disgrace, he had in mind to divorce her quietly.

[20] But after he had considered this, an angel of the Lord appeared to him in a dream and said, "Joseph son of David, do not be afraid to take Mary home as your wife, because what is conceived in her is from the Holy Spirit. [21] She will give birth to a son, and you are to give him the name Jesus, because he will save his people from their sins."

[22] All this took place to fulfill what the Lord had said through the prophet: [23] "The virgin will conceive and give birth to a son, and they will call him Immanuel" (which means "God with us").

[24] When Joseph woke up, he did what the angel of the Lord had commanded him and took Mary home as his wife.

[25] But he (Joseph) did not consummate their marriage until she gave birth to a son. And he gave him the name Jesus.

The Birth of the Baby in Bethlehem*

Luke 2:1-7

[1] In those days Caesar Augustus issued a decree that a census should be taken of the entire Roman world. [2] (This was the first census that took place while Quirinius was governor of Syria.) [3] And everyone went to their own town to register.

⁴ So Joseph also went up from the town of Nazareth in Galilee to Judea, to Bethlehem the town of David, because he belonged to the house and line of David. ⁵ He went there to register with Mary, who was pledged to be married to him and was expecting a child. ⁶ While they were there, the time came for the baby to be born, ⁷ and she gave birth to her firstborn, a son. She wrapped him in cloths and placed him in a manger, because there was no guest room available for them.

John 1:14

The Word became flesh and made his dwelling among us. We have seen his glory, the glory of the one and only Son, who came from the Father, full of grace and truth.

Shepherds and Angels (Luke 2:8–20)

⁸ And there were shepherds living out in the fields nearby, keeping watch over their flocks at night. ⁹ An angel of the Lord appeared to them, and the glory of the Lord shone around them, and they were terrified. ¹⁰ But the angel said to them, "Do not be afraid. I bring you good news that will cause great joy for all the people. ¹¹ Today in the town of David a Savior has been born to you; he is the Messiah, the Lord. ¹² This will be a sign to you: You will find a baby wrapped in cloths and lying in a manger."

Suddenly a great company of the heavenly host appeared with the angel, praising God and saying,

"Glory to God in the highest heaven,
  and on earth peace to those on whom his favor rests."

When the angels had left them and gone into heaven, the shepherds said to one another, "Let's go to Bethlehem and see this thing that has happened, which the Lord has told us about."

The Shepherds Visit

So they hurried off and found Mary and Joseph, and the baby, who was lying in the manger. [17] When they had seen him, they spread the word concerning what had been told them about this child, [18] and all who heard it were amazed at what the shepherds said to them. [19] But Mary treasured up all these things and pondered them in her heart. [20] The shepherds returned, glorifying and praising God for all the things they had heard and seen, which were just as they had been told.

Mary and Joseph meet Simeon and Anna in the Temple

Luke 2:21-38

On the eighth day, when it was time to circumcise the child, he was named Jesus, the name the angel had given him before he was conceived.

When the time came for the purification rites required by the Law of Moses, Joseph and Mary took him to Jerusalem to present him to the Lord [23] *(as it is written in the Law of the Lord, "Every firstborn male is to be consecrated to the Lord"),* [24] *and to offer a sacrifice in keeping with what is said in the Law of the Lord: "a pair of doves or two young pigeons."*

[25] *Now there was a man in Jerusalem called Simeon, who was righteous and devout. He was waiting for the consolation of Israel, and the Holy Spirit was on him.* [26] *It had been revealed to him by the Holy Spirit that he would not die before he had seen the Lord's Messiah.* [27] *Moved by the Spirit, he went into the temple courts. When the parents brought in the child Jesus to do for him what the custom of the Law required,* [28] *Simeon took him in his arms and praised God, saying:*

Simeon's Praise

[29] *"Sovereign Lord, as you have promised, you may now dismiss your servant in peace.*
[30] *For my eyes have seen your salvation,*
[31] *which you have prepared in the sight of all nations:*
[32] *a light for revelation to the Gentiles, and the glory of your people Israel."*

³³ *The child's father and mother marveled at what was said about him.* ³⁴ *Then Simeon blessed them and said to Mary, his mother: "This child is destined to cause the falling and rising of many in Israel, and to be a sign that will be spoken against,* ³⁵ *so that the thoughts of many hearts will be revealed. And a sword will pierce your own soul too."*

³⁶ *There was also a prophet, Anna, the daughter of Penuel, of the tribe of Asher. She was very old; she had lived with her husband seven years after her marriage,* ³⁷ *and then was a widow until she was eighty-four. She never left the temple but worshiped night and day, fasting and praying.* ³⁸ *Coming up to them at that very moment, she gave thanks to God and spoke about the child to all who were looking forward to the redemption of Jerusalem.*

King Herod and the Magi

Matthew 2:1-23

¹ *After Jesus was born in Bethlehem in Judea, during the time of King Herod, Magi from the east came to Jerusalem* ² *and asked, "Where is the one who has been born king of the Jews? We saw his star when it rose and have come to worship him."*

³ *When King Herod heard this he was disturbed, and all Jerusalem with him.* ⁴ *When he had called together all the*

people's chief priests and teachers of the law, he asked them where the Messiah was to be born. [5] "In Bethlehem in Judea," they replied, "for this is what the prophet has written:

[6] " 'But you, Bethlehem, in the land of Judah,
   are by no means least among the rulers of Judah;
for out of you will come a ruler
   who will shepherd my people Israel.' "

[7] Then Herod called the Magi secretly and found out from them the exact time the star had appeared. [8] He sent them to Bethlehem and said, "Go and search carefully for the child. As soon as you find him, report to me, so that I too may go and worship him."

The Magi Follow the Star to the Christ Child

[9] After they had heard the king, they went on their way, and the star they had seen when it rose went ahead of them until it stopped over the place where the child was. [10] When they saw the star, they were overjoyed. [11] On coming to the house, they saw the child with his mother Mary, and they bowed down and worshiped him. Then they opened their treasures and presented him with gifts of gold, frankincense and myrrh. [12] And having been warned in a dream not to go back to Herod, they returned to their country by another route.

Jesus' Family Flees Herod's Wrath

[13] *When they had gone, an angel of the Lord appeared to Joseph in a dream. "Get up," he said, "take the child and his mother and escape to Egypt. Stay there until I tell you, for Herod is going to search for the child to kill him."*

[14] *So he got up, took the child and his mother during the night and left for Egypt,* [15] *where he stayed until the death of Herod. And so was fulfilled what the Lord had said through the prophet: "Out of Egypt I called my son."*

[16] *When Herod realized that he had been outwitted by the Magi, he was furious, and he gave orders to kill all the boys in Bethlehem and its vicinity who were two years old and under, in accordance with the time he had learned from the Magi.* [17] *Then what was said through the prophet Jeremiah was fulfilled:*

[18] *"A voice is heard in Ramah,*
   weeping and great mourning,
Rachel weeping for her children
   and refusing to be comforted,
   because they are no more."

After Herod died, an angel of the Lord appeared in a dream to Joseph in Egypt [20] *and said, "Get up, take the child and his mother and go to the land of Israel, for those who were trying to take the child's life are dead."*

Jesus Is Raised in Nazareth

²¹ *So he got up, took the child and his mother and went to the land of Israel.* ²² *But when he heard that Archelaus was reigning in Judea in place of his father Herod, he was afraid to go there. Having been warned in a dream, he withdrew to the district of Galilee,* ²³ *and he went and lived in a town called Nazareth. So was fulfilled what was said through the prophets, that he would be called a Nazarene.*

Luke 2:39-40

³⁹ *When Joseph and Mary had done everything required by the Law of the Lord, they returned to Galilee to their own town of Nazareth.* ⁴⁰ *And the child grew and became strong; he was filled with wisdom, and the grace of God was on him.*

Certain books, videos, and studies were especially influential in my research.

The Jesus I Never Knew, Philip Yancey
In the Fullness of Time: A Historian Looks at Christmas, Easter, and the Early Church, Paul Maier
Focus on the Family Video, *Herod the Great, Jesus the King: The True Christmas Story*, Ray Vander Laan
Stories Behind the Great Traditions of Christmas, Ace Collins
The writings of Bob Deffinbaugh, Th.M
Jesus the One and Only, Beth Moore

Sources for Christmas Carol Research
The sources for the carol research are listed below, except for a few instances when I've made more specific references in endnotes.2

Ace Collins, *Stories Behind the Best-Loved Songs of Christmas* (Grand Rapids, MI: Zondervan, 2001).

Ernest K. Emurian, *Living Stories of Famous Hymns* (Grand Rapids, MI: Baker, 1955).

Christopher Idle, *Christmas Carols and Their Stories* (Batavia, IL: Lion Publishing Corporation, 1988).

Dale V. Nobbman, *The Christmas Music Companion Fact Book. The New Oxford Book of Carols*, Hugh Keyte and Andrew Parrott, eds. (New York: Oxford Press, 1992).

Virginia Reynolds, *The Spirit of Christmas: A History of Best-Loved Carols* (White Plains, NY: Peter Pauper Press, Inc., 2000).

Endnotes

1. Dr. Thomas Holmes, Dr. Richard Rahe, "Life Change Units." www.prcn.org/next/stress.html

2. Dale V. Nobbman, *The Christmas Music Companion Fact Book* (Anaheim Hills, CA: Centerstream Publishing, 2000), 56.

3. W. E. Vine, Merrill F. Unger, William White, Jr., *Vine's Complete Expository Dictionary of Old and New Testament Words* (Nashville, TN: Thomas Nelson, 1984), 381.

Beth Moore, *Jesus the One and Only* (Nashville, TN: LifeWay Press, 2000), 4.

4. Ralph Gower, *The New Manners and Customs of Bible Times* (Chicago, IL: Moody, 1987), 132–41.

5. Phillip Yancey, *The Jesus I Never Knew* (Grand Rapids, MI: Zondervan, 1995), 37.

6. Stephen C. Fehr, *The Washington Post*. November 27, 1994.

7. Paul Maier, *In the Fullness of Time: A Historian Looks at Christmas, Easter, and the Early Church*, 32.

Ray Vander Laan & Focus on the Family Video, *Herod the Great, Jesus the King: The True Christmas Story* (Grand Rapids, MI: Zondervan, 1999).

8. Ace Collins, *Stories Behind the Great Traditions of Christmas* (Grand Rapids, MI: Zondervan, 2003), 70–75; Walsh, 23–24.

9. http://www.silentnightmuseum.org/index.htm; Bill Egan,"SILENT NIGHT: The Song Heard 'Round The World," silentnight.web.za/history; "Joseph Mohr Gallery," Welcome.to/SilentNightMuseum

10. Egan, "War and Remembrance: The Truce of 1914," Welcome.to/SilentNightMuseum; Walsh, 118–119.

11. Yancey, *The Jesus I Never Knew*, 35–36.

12. Max Lucado, *One Incredible Moment* (Nashville, TN: J. Countryman/Thomas Nelson, 2001), 38.

13. Collins, *Stories,* 25–26; 115–116.

14. Bob Deffinbaugh, "Two Incredible Journeys (Matthew 2:1–23)"; "Responses to the Revelation of the Coming of the King (Matthew 2:1–12, 16–18)," http://www.bible.org/

15. Winifred Walker, *All the Plants of the Bible* (Garden City, NY: Doubleday & Company, Inc., 1979), 78–79.

16. *Ibid.*, 122–123.

17. Deffinbaugh, "Two Incredible Journeys (Matthew 2:1–23)"; Maier, 51–61; Walsh, 40–41.

18. Vander Laan & Focus on the Family Video (video production).

19. Joseph J. Walsh, *Were They Wise Men or Kings? The Book of Christmas Questions,* (Louisville, KY: Westminster John Knox Press, 2001), 44–45; Daniel B. Wallace, Th.M., Ph.D., "The Birth of Jesus Christ," http://www.bible.org/pageg.asp?page_id=656/; Deffinbaugh, "Two Incredible Journeys (Matthew 2:1–23)," in "Studies in the Gospel of Matthew," http://www.bible.org/page.asp?page_id=1054/; Deffinbaugh, "Responses to the Revelation of the Coming of the King (Matthew 2:1–12, 16–18)," http://www.bible.org/

20. Deffinbaugh, "Two Incredible Journeys (Matthew 2:1–23)."

21. *Ibid*, "Christmas Faith (Matthew 1:18—2:23)," http://www.bible.org/page.asp?page_id=670/; Maier, 64; Wallace, "The Birth of Jesus Christ," http://www.bible.org/pageg.asp?page_id=656/

22. Walsh, 29–30; Collins, *Stories*, 138–43.

23. Deffinbaugh, "Responses," http://www.bible.org.

24. Ace Collins, *Stories*, 41–45; Lori Walburg, *The Legend of the*

Candy Cane (Grand Rapids, MI: Zonderkidz, 1997); Jane Jarrell, Mary Beth Lagerborg, *Great Books to Read and Fun Things to Do with Them* (Grand Rapids, MI: Zondervan, 2000), 128–30; Walker, 96–97.